Helping yourself

with self-hypnosis

Helping yourself
with self-hypnosis

A MODERN GUIDE
TO SELF-IMPROVEMENT
AND SUCCESSFUL LIVING

by

▲ Frank S. Caprio, M. D.

and

▲ Joseph R. Berger

Prentice-Hall, Inc.
Englewood Cliffs, N. J.

Reward Edition. . . . .March, 1974
Fifteenth Printing. . . . .August, 1982

This book is a reference work based on research by
the author. The opinions expressed herein are not
necessarily those of or endorsed by the Publisher.

It matters not how strait the gate,
How charged with punishment the scroll,
I am the master of my fate;
I am the captain of my soul.

—WILLIAM ERNEST HENLEY

Foreword

▲ As Executive Director of the American Institute of Hypnosis, I have had the pleasure of giving lectures and demonstrations to thousands of physicians throughout the United States and in many other countries on the amazing phenomenon of self-hypnosis. Because of my great interest in this fascinating subject, I am delighted that a man of Dr. Caprio's intelligence and experience has undertaken to write a book on autohypnosis aimed at the layman. Furthermore, his co-author, Joseph R. Berger, is both a good friend and a former student, who has not only distinguished himself in the field of psychology but in the field of medical writing as well.

I am especially pleased with this book, because it has always been my belief that the average intelligence of the American public has been grossly underestimated. There will, of course, be some criticism from those members of the medical profession who believe that no one should be educated in medicine except the physician. However, I agree with the many physicians who believe that the proper education of all the people regarding the fundamentals of good health, both mental and physical, is an end result greatly to be desired.

It is doubtful if there is a citizen in the United States today who has not at one time or another attempted some form of self-medication, whether it be an aspirin for a headache or a cathartic for constipation. And, certainly, a well-informed public in the field of medicine is to be desired. This book goes a long way toward eradicating the many ridiculous misconceptions which exist concerning hypnosis. Chapter One, dealing with facts and fallacies connected with hypnosis, explains these misconceptions in plain, everyday language which everyone can understand. This chapter, by itself, is more than worth the price of the whole book.

In my opinion, this book is exceptionally well written. I recommend it as a guide to laymen, and it should also prove interesting reading for both physicians and dentists who are utilizing hypnosis in their practices.

WILLIAM J. BRYAN, JR., M.D.
Executive Director
American Institute of Hypnosis
Los Angeles, California

Acknowledgments

━━━━━━━━━━━━━━━━━━━━━━━━━━━━━━━━━━━━━

▲ In addition to acknowledging our indebtedness to our wives, who have been a tremendous help with the typing and retyping of the manuscript, we would also like to express our thanks to Dr. William Bryan for consenting to write the Foreword and to Melvin Powers for reading the book in manuscript form and offering many valuable suggestions.

Contents

CHAPTER   PAGE

**Introduction—SELF-HYPNOSIS: The new way to
successful living** **1**

Better health, more happiness, greater success are attainable goals. How this book came about. The purpose of the book. All hypnosis is self-hypnosis. Self-hypnosis has unlimited potentialities. A few examples of what self-hypnosis has been able to do. Self-hypnosis enables you to discover and develop your new self. You can enjoy better health through self-hypnosis. Self-hypnosis will help you achieve personality-maturity. Successful planning. Self-hypnosis also improves your love life. How to use this book to advantage. Summing up.

1   The secret of the "hypnotic state" **11**

Definition of hypnosis. What is hypnotism? Origin of the word. There are two kinds of hypnosis. What is meant by the "hypnotic state"? How and why hypnosis works. Theories of hypnosis. Common fallacies and facts. Hypnosis versus self-hypnosis. Self-hypnosis in our daily lives. Hypnosis and self-hypnosis: forces for good. Self-hypnosis works automatically. 10 main points in chapter one.

**2   The 4-A's method of self-hypnosis: a step-by-step
plan** **25**

First, decide what you want self-hypnosis to do for you. The 4-A's method of self-hypnosis. How to achieve self-hypnosis in the waking state. How to rouse yourself out of the hypnotic state. Always keep this in mind. A word of caution. Regarding emotional problems. An added advantage: the experience of being hypnotized. Chapter highlights.

CHAPTER   **PAGE**

3   How to communicate with your subconscious mind   40

Self-hypnosis can release hidden potentials within you. Start by learning to plan your time and energy wisely. The advantages of intelligent planning. Your subconscious mind. Communicating with your subconscious mind. Study your dreams—they can tell you much about your subconscious self. How to make your subconscious mind work for you. Self-hypnosis can increase your powers of concentration. Summary.

4   The amazing power of self-hypnosis for daily health and weight-control **57**

Establishing good health-habits with self-hypnosis. Daily health reminders. Self-hypnosis: The modern approach to successful weight-control. The amazing Hypno-Diet. Overeating is a form of "psychic suicide." Obesity and emotional problems. A nine-step program for weight-reduction. What losing weight the self-hypnosis way will do for you. Salient points.

5   Self-hypnosis, smoking, and alcohol **74**

Facts about smoking. 14 suggestions to follow—if you want to stop smoking. The problem of alcoholism. Subconscious causes of excessive drinking. Use self-hypnosis to help find and remove the cause of excessive drinking. To sum up.

6   The hypnotic road to restful sleep **87**

Many factors cause sleeplessness. How to induce restful sleep. Basic points to remember.

7   What self-hypnosis can do to make your sex-life more exciting **94**

Start with an inventory of your sex-life. What to ask yourself. What to tell yourself. Self-hypnosis can help you develop the capacity to accept and give love. Frigidity can be overcome with self-hypnosis. Self-hypnosis and the single girl. The use of self-hypnosis for the problem of impotence. Summing it all up.

8 You can overcome nervous tension, pain, and chronic tiredness with self-hypnosis 109

Learn all about "tension." How to control tension-reactions. Alleviation of pain with hypnosis. Hypnosis and the medical world. What you should know about "nervous fatigue." Self-therapeutic suggestions for the release of tension-fatigue. What the ability to relax will mean. The worry habit and what you can do about it. Develop a sense of humor—it's a tension-reducer. Salient points.

9 Master your emotions through self-hypnosis 119

How to control fear through self-hypnosis. How to use self-hypnosis to conquer a bad temper. You can relax away sick emotions. Self-hypnosis and morbid fears. How to overcome the fear of air travel with self-hypnosis. Techniques to overcome fear of flying. Key things to remember.

10 You can defeat mental depression and unhappy moods with self-hypnosis 134

Analyze the nature and cause of your unhappy moods. What you should know about mental depression. Use posthypnotic suggestion to divert your mind from yourself. Self-hypnotic suggestions for banishing the "blues." Points to remember.

11 How to create for yourself a new personality and a happier life 144

Just what is meant by "personality"? Try to understand what made you what you are. Can you change your personality? The self-hypnosis approach to personality change. How to acquire personality-magnetism. While you're at it, learn to improve your vocabulary. Steps for improving your vocabulary. Develop a tolerant personality with self-hypnosis. Enlist the cooperation of your friends for personality-improvement. Self-hypnosis improves your memory and ability to learn. Summary.

12 How to achieve hypnotic power, control, and influence over others 159

What getting along with people by using self-hypnosis can do for you. When you are using self-hypnosis keep the

12 **How to achieve hypnotic power, control, and influence over others (continued)**

following in mind. Self-hypnosis enhances salesmanship ability. Visual reminders. Essential points to remember.

13 **Self-hypnosis techniques to make a success of your marriage** 167

How to attain greater happiness in marriage through self-hypnosis. Twelve helpful suggestions for husbands. Twelve helpful suggestions for wives. A marriage that was saved with self-hypnosis. Self-hypnosis can also make you a better parent. Summary.

14 **Using hypnotic magic to stay young and live longer** 177

You are as old as you feel. Make happier living your goal. A theory of aging: mind over body. Let your work become your hobby. Hypnosis and religion. Self-hypnosis makes prayer more effective. I believe. What to remember.

15 **Richer living through new thought patterns** 189

You and heredity. Making the most of each day. Twenty-five guaranteed dividends. A reinforced suggestion.

Epilogue 199

Bibliography 201

Index 207

SELF-HYPNOSIS:

The new way

to successful living

▲ Self-hypnosis can bring great benefits to
your life—more energy, better health, lasting peace of mind,
success and happiness.

**Better health, more happiness,
greater success are attainable goals**

The pursuit of health, happiness and success is a universal
goal. Everyone would like to enjoy good health. Everyone would
like to be happy. Everyone would like to experience the satisfaction of having made a success of his life.

We are of the opinion that the person who has a sincere and
genuine desire to improve himself, his health, his thinking and
way of life can bring this about through his own efforts, provided
of course he is given some guidance as to what he needs to know,
where to begin in this over-all plan of self-improvement.

We have tried to avoid writing a book on psychiatry for the
layman. Instead we attempted merely to point out the impor-

tance of correct thinking, how the mind influences the way we feel, what we can do to achieve inner strength, to survive adversities and how we can improve ourselves in every way so that we can enjoy fuller and richer living.

We all have greater mind-power than we realize. Everything within reason is humanly possible. We need never consider ourselves failures or remain unhappy. There is much that we can do to correct and improve our situation in life.

How this book came about

This book was inspired by the public's response to an article, "Think Your Fears Away," which the authors had published in *The American Weekly*, January 31, 1960. From the letters received, we assumed that there must be thousands of people looking for guidance as to *how they can help themselves; how they can improve themselves and achieve a fuller, richer life.*

The purpose of the book

Our purpose in writing this book is to convince you—by having you prove it to yourself—that you possess certain self-hypnotic powers—that self-hypnosis can do for you the things *you want it to do.* It can be a tremendous weapon at your command, enabling you to manage everyday situations wisely.

That your Mind is the MASTER OF YOUR LIFE is the basic message of this book. It is founded on the proven philosophy that TO LIVE RIGHT YOU MUST THINK RIGHT. *How you live is how you use your mind.*

All hypnosis is self-hypnosis

The authors, having engaged in a five-year research project with actual patients to see what hypnosis can do, concluded that since all hypnosis is self-hypnosis, the average person can be taught the techniques of self-hypnosis to increase his confidence, his zest for living and other real accomplishments of his choosing. The individual allows himself to be influenced by his own thoughts or thought suggestions.

"Actually you hypnotize yourself, the power being supplied by your own intelligence and concentration," according to Melvin Powers, well-known hypnotist and authority on the subject. "The hypnotist," to quote Powers, "is merely 'the instrument' through which you are able to reach a state of hypnosis." He guides the subject into the hypnotic state but in reality the subject by his own efforts achieves the hypnotic state. If the subject did not wish to be hypnotized, it would be impossible for the hypnotist to put him in the hypnotic state. Thus we see that the subject is always in control of the hypnotic state and also controls the depth of the response.

Self-hypnosis has unlimited potentialities

Many great achievements have come about in the past through hypnosis, but the science is just coming out of the dark age in which it was considered the work of the devil or a ridiculous stage act. It is no longer regarded as black magic. Hypnosis today is a dignified science. It has gained worldwide interest and holds a recognized place in the medical profession.

Although the practice of hypnosis can be traced back as far as the era of primitive healers, the development and application of self-hypnosis is a relatively new phenomenon.

Because human beings are so autosuggestible, self-hypnosis can do wonderful things. You can make your subconscious mind work to your advantage. The subconscious mind plays a far more important role in daily life than most realize.

"Self-hypnosis plays a valuable role in a process which makes it easier for an individual to discover and understand the workings of his own body and mind, learn the factors which basically cause his own distress and learn how to control them." This is how Dr. Milton Erickson, dean of the American Medical Hypnotists, described the phenomenon of self-hypnosis.

Too many people today are relying entirely on pills to relax them—*pharmaceutical* relaxation. We don't minimize the value which tranquilizers have in those cases where drug therapy is indicated. We are, however, aware of the many people who depend upon them, and use them indiscriminately when it is far better for them to achieve autorelaxation—a natural form of relaxation through self-hypnosis.

A few examples of what self-hypnosis has been able to do

An artist who loved to paint, but who lacked self-confidence, has become a prize-winner several times over after learning the technique of self-hypnosis.

A once-successful writer, convinced that he was all washed up, was trained to relax as he writes—and to look more deeply into himself. He now has a best seller on the list.

A famous man who suffered acute anxiety when he had to address a group was taught the technique of hypnotic autorelaxation which enabled him to speak without fear.

These are not isolated cases. We have had many similar ones. In the modern world of the cold war, tensions seem to be a part of us and it takes real concentration to keep these tensions from affecting our whole outlook. But it can be done through self-hypnosis.

Much has been written of the results achieved in alleviating the pain of childbirth and dental surgery, by the use of hypnosis and the power of posthypnotic suggestion to cure obesity, alcoholism and excessive smoking. However, one does not have to be obese, in pain, alcoholic or even neurotic to benefit from hypnosis or self-hypnosis.

One of our greatest successes has been our work with children and teenagers, helping them straighten out their thought responses before they grow into anxiety-laden adults. Young people in school can be taught to relax without worry before an examination. They can then enjoy the challenge of the test, thinking and remembering the answers they already know without the usual tension.

Self-hypnosis enables you to discover and develop your new self

You will begin to believe in yourself, acquire confidence you never had before. For the first time in your life you will experience a feeling of self-importance.

Thinking positively about yourself is the first step in any self-improvement program. In becoming a new person you will begin to develop normal self-love, self-respect, self-confidence and inner contentment. Your future will depend on this *inner self*—the way you think about yourself. You cannot expect self-hypnosis to do wonderful things for you unless you first succeed in liking yourself—the new self—the self you want to be. The achievement of this first goal will lead to the successful attainment of other equally important goals.

You can enjoy better health through self-hypnosis

It is claimed that approximately 60 to 75 per cent of the ills people complain about are *psychosomatic*. This would mean that the *emotional factor* plays a very important role in illness. The late Dr. Schindler in his book *How to Live 365 Days a Year* * describes how a negative mental attitude can cause illness. If emotionally induced illness is as prevalent as it is claimed to be, then it would seem logical that the control of one's emotions, or

---

* John Schindler, M.D., *How to Live 365 Days a Year* (Englewood Cliffs, N.J.: Prentice-Hall, Inc., 1954).

the improvement of one's attitude, accomplished through self-hypnosis, would do much to prevent the development of pyscho-somatic ailments. Self-hypnosis can also help the patient suffering from physical or organic illness by making him less apprehensive, more tolerant to discomfort, and increasing his will to live. What is self-hypnosis but the technique of influencing your own thinking to advantage—managing your emotions successfully at all times?

Many people become chronic health-complainers only because their symptom-complaints represent expressions of some inner unhappiness. The person who subjects himself to self-analysis, attempting to uproot the cause of his unhappiness (following this with auto-posthypnotic suggestion as a remedy) is less apt to become a hypochondriac.

Self-hypnosis enables you to become a better patient in time of an emergency illness. It enables you to be less fearful of an operation, to become more cooperative and to assume an optimistic outlook during your convalescence.

Self-hypnosis will help you achieve personality-maturity

Personality-maturity implies many things. It represents balanced living, wisdom, intelligence, good moral character, kindness, a code of ethics, a healthy sense of values, the ability to get along with people, a gladness to be alive, the courage to face reality and adjust to adversities, a willingness to grow and be of service to others, a belief in the goodness of life. It means all these things and everything else that reflects that which is positive, good and acceptable to mankind.

A well-integrated personality is an asset in life. It gives you the fortitude to withstand misfortunes. People who are well adjusted are capable of doing good, of inspiring others to climb and achieve success. They console those who are in despair. We all benefit from the wisdom of those who have found the secret of maturity. But such a goal as personality-maturity is not acquired overnight. It requires persistent effort. It takes stick-to-it-tiveness. It means working at self-improvement every day. It entails learning, studying, listening, working, growing and developing self-confidence through accomplishments—achieving one goal at a time. You must know the kind of person you want to be before you become that person. It's a matter of reminding yourself from day to day of those personality assets you wish to acquire. Personality-maturity when you have it is like money in the bank, like owning a home without a mortgage. It is mind-health, mind-power.

Successful planning

Self-hypnosis enables you to plan and organize your time and daily activities to good advantage.

Much of your happiness and success in life depends upon your ability to use your time wisely and plan intelligently. Time is accessible to everyone. Going to bed every night knowing that you have devoted your time to doing something constructive, learning something new, improving yourself or planning for a particular goal, should bring you the kind of mental satisfaction that makes day-to-day living inspiring. It gives you a *joie de vivre* —a feeling that you are making yourself useful—giving meaning to life.

Self-hypnosis is synonymous with self-discipline. It means starting the day with a healthy attitude toward the responsibilities you must face as well as knowing how you are going to organize your time and energy for each particular day. To live without plans is to sail a ship without a compass. To build you must be guided by a set of plans. To work toward a given goal you must have organization.

Organization means knowing what you want out of life, what you don't want, what you expect from yourself and others, how you prefer to spend your time and what you must do to achieve your goals. It means thinking straight—positive thinking—rational thinking—thinking with a plan.

Once you have developed the ability to utilize time and energy wisely, you are ready to direct the power of self-hypnosis toward the achievement of your next goal.

Self-hypnosis also improves your love life

Through self-hypnosis you stand a better chance of finding love, giving love and sharing love. Love-happiness is an experience, a feeling within, a something you share. If you feel love in your heart, you are able to reflect it. It is easy to express something you feel. Love-happiness is essential to marriage-happiness. Self-hypnosis should enable you to become a lovable person, a better candidate for a happy marriage.

If you are already married, it should help you improve your relationship to your married partner. Self-discipline and self-control achieved through self-hypnotic techniques will act as a protection to your marriage. It will keep you and your married partner from saying unkind things to each other, from doing anything that will jeopardize your happiness. Self-hypnosis should enable you to enjoy the physical expression of love. It should make you more responsive, more receptive and a happy co-participant. A happy couple is one who enjoys a happy love-sex relationship. Happily married people get more out of life. They make better friends, better parents, and better citizens. Their happiness is contagious. Improve your love life and you will have achieved one of the important ingredients of successful living, for what is life without love? The Italians have a saying: "A meal without wine is like a day without sunshine." We can paraphrase it by saying, Life without love is like a flower without fragrance. Love is the *élan vital* of life; love is the *raison d'être* of life—the motivation behind everything that is good in the world. Love-happiness means life-happiness. Love is something you can develop, acquire, possess. It is a feeling that you can experience by planting the seeds of love in your mind, in your thinking, in everything you do. Love is an attitude of mind which you can develop through self-hypnosis. Learn to *think love in your mind and you will feel love in your heart.*

How to use this book to advantage

The knowledge you will have gained from reading and re-reading this book should convince you that self-hypnosis is simply a technique for developing greater self-discipline, helping you achieve your goals in life—self-hypnosis helps you to help yourself. When you have finished reading the book, resolve that you have just begun your new way to successful living.

Use the contents of this book to inspire you to better yourself in every way. Practice the techniques faithfully for achieving self-mastery.

Self-hypnosis gives you *mind-power.* It gives you the ability to convert acquired knowledge into *wisdom.*

If you make this book your guide to self-improvement you will be reaping the maximum benefit from all that you have learned.

Incidentally, we would like to inform the reader that if many of the case-illustrations seem to have something in common, it is only because we purposely made a point of acquainting each subject with the terminology of hypnosis. We encouraged each subject to use certain technical words and in many instances, we even phrased for him the posthypnotic suggestions he was to memorize and repeat. We did this merely to furnish him with a sample of the kind of thought-suggestions he should give himself which would be applicable to a specific problem. However, we recommend that if he preferred, he could formulate his own self-suggestions, expressing them in any way he desired.

Summing up

1. Self-hypnosis is a technique or method of utilizing the power of your own mind for self-improvement. It is a new approach to the solution of common everyday problems.

2. Once you have mastered the techniques of self-hypnosis you will be able to give yourself whatever specific constructive suggestions you desire to accept and follow.

Self-hypnosis will enable you to:

1. Think your morbid fears away.
2. Achieve a fuller, richer life.
3. Enjoy better physical and mental health.
4. Develop self-sufficiency and self-hypnotic confidence.
5. Plan wisely.
6. Make your subconscious mind work for you.
7. Acquire a deeper understanding of your inner self.
8. Alleviate tension.
9. Break undesirable habits.
10. Attain a mature sense of values.
11. Become the kind of person you want to be.
12. Improve your love life.

Chapter One

The secret of
the "hypnotic state"

●●●●●●●●●●●●●●●●●●●●●●●●●●●●●●●●●●●●●●●

▲ The authors feel that for you to under-
stand the mechanism of self-hypnosis properly and have self-
hypnosis work for you successfully, it is essential that you have
some knowledge of what we mean by "hypnosis," the different
theories about it, the various fallacies and facts of it and how
hypnosis and self-hypnosis act as forces for good.

Definition of hypnosis

Hypnosis may be defined as a sleep-like condition produced
by the hypnotist in a subject who *allows* himself to accept and
respond to certain specific suggestions.

Leslie LeCron, psychologist and lecturer on hypnotism, describes hypnosis as "The uncritical acceptance of a suggestion by
the patient in a trance." Andrew Salter, author of *What Is
Hypnosis?*, is of the opinion that hypnosis is nothing more than
"a conditioned reflex." Nevertheless most professionals in the
field regard hypnosis as an *exaggerated form of suggestibility*, or
what some writers refer to as *hypersuggestibility*.

What is hypnotism?

The science and art of inducing this sleep-like state in a subject is known as hypnotism.

Origin of the word

The term "hypnosis" is derived from the name of the Greek god of sleep "Hypnos" and was coined by an English physician, Dr. James Braid, in 1843. Incidentally, we believe that it is an unfortunate term since it conveys the erroneous impression that hypnosis is the same as sleep. Actually, hypnosis as already defined, means increased receptivity to suggestion. It has been discovered that suggestion has a more profound effect when the subject is in a hypnotic state.

There are two kinds of hypnosis

· 1. Hetero-hypnosis: The induction of the hypnotic state in a subject by someone else (the hypnotist—sometimes called the "operator").

2. Autohypnosis or self-hypnosis: The induction of the hypnotic state by oneself.

What is meant by the "hypnotic state"?

The hypnotic state is a condition that is somewhat similar to sleep. Hypnosis and sleep are not the same thing. In the hypnotic state the reflexes are present. In natural sleep reflexes are diminished or absent.

The hypnotic state may be compared to a dream-like state. The person in a hypnotic state is self-absorbed as if in fantasy. The hypnotic state has also been likened to a state of absentmindedness, or a state of dissociation of consciousness in which the subject is partially withdrawn from reality. Actually, the subject is fully aware of what is happening and is extremely alert.

How and why hypnosis works

Hypnosis is made possible because all human beings are *suggestible.*

SUGGESTION is the key to hypnotism.

We are all susceptible to being influenced by other persons in varying degrees. Consequently, hypnotic phenomena can be demonstrated in practically *everyone.* In some instances the person has to be *conditioned* to techniques of hypnosis and self-hypnosis. Everyone is influenced by his own thinking. It is this autosuggestible component in all of us that also makes self-hypnosis possible.

Because of everyone's susceptibility to suggestion, Emile Coué, the French psychologist, gained wide recognition and popularity as a result of his "Day by day in every way—I am feeling better and better" approach to problems.

We have all heard the expression "You can talk yourself into or out of anything," depending upon what you really want to do. In the same way you can *think* yourself into or out of anything, depending upon the kind of suggestions you give yourself. Self-suggestion is the magic key to self-improvement.

There is nothing mysterious about hypnosis. Its application is based solely on the known psychological relationship between the conscious and the subconscious minds. The subconscious, having no power to reason, accepts and acts upon any fact or suggestion given to it by the conscious mind.

The hypnotist asks the subject to accept suggestions uncritically so that the reasoning, analytic qualities of the mind are suspended and the suggestion goes unchanged to the subconscious.

This technique of hypnosis is the method used to bypass the conscious mind. It is strengthened by concentrating the conscious attention upon a single object or thought.

The depth of hypnosis is dependent upon increased suggestibility. The hypnotist requests the person to concentrate his attention upon a whirling disk, a flashing light or some object that will tire his vision. He then suggests that the subject relax. He tells him his lids are becoming heavy and his eyes will close. With each suggestion the person accepts without a conscious challenge, the hypnotist can more directly establish a contact with the subconscious mind.

Theories of hypnosis

There are many controversial theories regarding the exact nature of hypnosis. Professor H. Bernheim, one of the earliest pioneers in the field of hypnosis, who induced hypnosis over 10,000 times, attributed the entire phenomena to *suggestibility*. Charcot maintained that hypnosis was merely a manifestation of *hysteria*. Pavlov believed that hypnosis and sleep were identical. Dr. S. J. Van Pelt adheres to the theory that hypnosis is no more than a *super-concentration of the mind*.

Sigmund Freud, on the other hand, concluded that the mechanism of hypnosis could be explained on the basis of *emotional rapport* (transference), which the subject experiences toward the hypnotist as a parent-substitute. He believed that not all subjects were hypnotizable, that in hypnosis the subject develops too great a dependency on the hypnotist and for this reason abandoned hypnosis in favor of psychoanalysis. However, we now know this is not true. The hypnotherapist stresses the need for the patient to become emotionally *self-sustaining*. He uses the same technique of counter-transference that the psychoanalyst uses to offset the patient's dependency.

Common fallacies and facts

There are many misconceptions about hypnosis. Before a person is hypnotized or employs self-hypnosis he should acquire preliminary information as to what *isn't* true about hypnosis so that his fears about it may be allayed. He is more apt to respond successfully if he is prepared properly for hypnosis by knowing clearly what to anticipate. We contend that the more knowledge a person possesses about the subject, the more favorable the result.

The following represents some of the more common fallacies which many people harbor. These serious misconceptions serve only as a hindrance to successful hypnosis. They came about as a result of erroneous impressions conveyed to the public via sensational stage demonstrations, over the radio and on television. Many novels and articles have been written about hypnosis which contain inaccurate information. Here are a few examples of some mistaken ideas about hypnosis.

The Fallacy:

A hypnotist is a person gifted with unusual Svengali-like or mysterious magic power.

The Fact:

▲ Hypnotists do not possess any unusual or mystic powers. A hypnotist is a person who knows that his subject actually hypnotizes himself. The hypnotist is merely a person who has learned or perhaps mastered the science and art of *effective suggestion*. He teaches the subject how to bring about or self-induce the hypnotic state. Hypnotism has sometimes been called the "manipulation of the imagination."

The Fallacy:

A person in a hypnotic state may not be easily awakened and may remain in that state for a long time.

The Fact:

▲ The hypnotic state is similar to becoming completely absorbed in a movie or a book. In other words, it represents a concentration of attention.

No one has ever remained indefinitely in a hypnotic state. The hypnotist or subject terminates the hypnotic state at will. It is as simple as opening one's eyes. The subject eventually awakens from what is known as "hypnotic sleep." Any fear of not awakening is not warranted. There has never been a case in which the subject did not return to the waking state.

The Fallacy:

Hypnosis effects a cure in just one or two sessions.

The Fact:

▲ In many instances one or two sessions of hypnosis may enable a person to break a habit. However, in the majority of cases it requires a number of sessions before a favorable result is obtained.

The Fallacy:

Many people cannot be hypnotized.

The Fact:

▲ Ninety per cent of all people can be hypnotized. You cannot hypnotize a feeble-minded person. It takes imagination and a willingness to cooperate—a willingness to accept suggestions. Reinforced sessions make the subject more hypnotizable. Children, incidentally, respond well to hypnotic techniques. The best subject is the person who has a definite reason or motivation for wanting to be hypnotized. The ability to be hypnotized successfully lies within yourself. It is dependent upon your ability to overcome your resistance to hypnosis. This resistance may be conscious or unconscious.

To be hypnotized, (1) you must *want* to be hypnotized; (2) you must have confidence in the hypnotist; (3) you must train your mind to *accept* suggestion. Dave Elman, who conducts courses in hypnosis for physicians and dentists, includes a fourth requirement—absolute freedom from fear. He adds, "Remove fear—the biggest block of all—and you'll be able to hypnotize one hundred people out of a hundred."

The Fallacy:

Under hypnosis you are apt to do anything—good or bad— you are like a slave who obeys his master automatically, irrespective of what you are told to do.

The Fact:

▲ Under hypnosis the subject will not do anything contrary to his moral principles. He will not commit an antisocial act. He has the power to select only the suggestions he is willing to accept. He will reject any improper suggestions.

According to Dr. Roy M. Dorcus, Professor of Psychology at the University of California at Los Angeles, "A hypnotized patient is never in anybody else's power. He won't go into a trance unless he wants to. He won't do anything unless he wants to. And he won't stay in a trance if he wants to come out of it."

The Fallacy:

Hypnosis means being put to sleep and not being aware of one's surroundings.

The Fact:

▲ Hypnosis does not necessarily mean falling asleep. Under hypnosis awareness is increased. If the subject does fall asleep, it is only because he himself was completely relaxed, and wanted to sleep; he will ultimately awaken refreshed.

The Fallacy:

A person has to be put into a deep stage of hypnosis before he can be helped.

The Fact:

▲ You need not be in a deep stage of hypnosis to benefit from hypnosis. Many excellent results are being obtained by utilizing the beneficial suggestible state of light induction.

The Fallacy:

Hypnosis will not help persons suffering from deep-seated sexual problems.

The Fact:

▲ Hypnosis has proved effective in helping many persons overcome sexual problems. Many cases of impotence and frigidity, as well as other sexual disorders, have been reported as responding successfully to hypnotherapy.

The Fallacy:

Persons who are easily hypnotized are weak-willed.

The Fact:

▲ The more intelligent and imaginative the person the easier it is to hypnotize him. You don't have to be "weak-minded" to be hypnotized.

The Fallacy:

A hypnotist can induce a person to commit a crime.

The Fact:

▲ A hypnotist cannot induce a person to commit a crime or any illegal act.

The Fallacy:

Being hypnotized means lapsing into a state of uncon-sciousness.

The Fact:

▲ Being hypnotized, even in a deep state, does not mean lapsing into a state of unconsciousness. Under hypnosis you are aware of everything that is going on.

Hypnosis versus self-hypnosis

As we already explained in the introduction, all hypnosis is self-hypnosis. In hypnosis the subject responds to the suggestions of the hypnotist. The subject *permits* the hypnotist to bring about a state of calmness and relaxation because he, the subject, *desires* this mental state.

Hypnosis involves (1) motivation, (2) relaxation and (3) suggestion.

In self-hypnosis, the relaxation is *self-induced*, followed by the hypnotic state. It is the influence of our own minds over our bodies. By inducing our own hypnotic state, we heighten our suggestibility and are then capable of influencing our body functions, of experiencing tranquility without the use of drugs. Or, we may give ourselves specific chosen suggestions in the hypnotic state (posthypnotic suggestion). The actual techniques of self-hypnosis will be discussed in the next chapter.

The phenomena of hypnosis and self-hypnosis explain many of our publicized miracles of faith cures.

Self-hypnosis is really a form of *psychic healing* accomplished through the voluntary *acceptance and application of one's own suggestions.*

Self-hypnosis in our daily lives

Every one of us practices some form of self-hypnosis unknowingly. For instance, we find ourselves being irresistibly coerced, persuaded or influenced by the suggestions of others. It would be impossible to estimate the extent or role which hypnotic influences play in our everyday thinking. Our life is constantly changing because of what we see, hear or tell ourselves. Suggestibility is a common denominator in the psychology of human behavior. Many of the things we believe are accepted on faith. We believe them only because we *want* to believe them. Some of us, of course, are more suggestible than others.

For example, the compulsion to buy what we see and want (oniomania) operates on the principle of hypnotic influences. Something tells us we *must* have it. The picture of a delicious piece of pie on the restaurant mirror, travel pictures of Venice or Paris, a beautiful girl modeling a swim suit are examples of *hypnotic visual appeal*. A suggestive picture of a Florida home with palm trees and a boat tied up at a private dock, with persuasive descriptions of how easy it is to own is another example of "let us make up your mind for you."

A manifestation of self-hypnosis is disguised in the phenomenon of being in love or falling in love. Proof of the interrelationship between hypnosis and love is evidenced in Dr. Bernard Hollander's observation:*

> One of the best examples of the effect of suggestion to the extent of its becoming an obsession is that of a person who has fallen in love. It is as powerful in its mental and bodily effects as hypnotism. The man or woman who has induced this state of mind exercises a strong fascination over the subject, resulting in complete blindness to the attractions of all other persons and to the physical and mental defects of the object of adoration. Men in love

* Bernard Hollander, M.D., *Methods and Use of Hypnosis & Self-Hypnosis* (Hollywood, Calif.: Wilshire Book Co., 1957), p. 118.

sometimes change the habits of a lifetime, break with their own relations, dismiss their most faithful servants, ruin themselves financially, give up their club and smoking, and may even change their politics and religion. Simultaneously with these mental changes there are certain physical symptoms. In the presence of the object of infatuation a gentle languor pervades the frame; the respiration becomes sighing; the blood rushes to the head, causing a flushing of the countenance. Accompanying this is a great confusion of thought and language. Particularly in young persons, and when very acute there may be loss of appetite and insomnia. There is usually a disposition to violent palpitation of the heart and a sensation at times as if the heart had been displaced upward into the larynx. Persons in love become highly sensitive to each other's feelings. The slightest inattention, or a greeting less warm than usual, will cause serious agitation, worry, misery, lasting for hours or even days. They become moody and avoid society. If the neglect continues they grow pale and thin, morbid thoughts of self-destruction may arise, and sometimes homicidal impulses at the sight of a rival have been known to occur. On the other hand, a contact of the hands, and even more so of the lips or cheeks, though the action last but a second, may excite feelings of exaltation and happiness of an enduring character. There is no hypnotist who can produce such complex results at once as are manifest in a person who has "fallen in love."

Dr. George C. Kingsbury, author of *The Practice of Hypnotic Suggestion*, describes how Indian fakirs resort to *self-hypnosis* by fixing their eyes on a selected object, and how our own American Indians in Dakota would put themselves in the hypnotic state while performing their "ghost dance" and finally fall asleep. He mentions the monks of Mount Athos who hypnotized themselves by looking steadily at their own navels.

Everyone can prove to himself through practice that he is capable of hypnotizing himself. Some of us allow ourselves to relax and fall asleep reading a book or listening to soft music. Others accomplish the same effect through conscious auto-suggestion and autoconditioning. Building up our own self-confidence in a way is a form of self-hypnosis.

Remember that everyone can develop into a good subject with sufficient motivation and practice.

Hypnosis and self-hypnosis: forces for good

As you know, the public has always been fascinated by the subject of hypnotism. Fortunately, people are becoming more and more educated as to the myths and facts of hypnosis. So-called "stage hypnosis" is becoming extinct, like the old-time vaudeville. Today current magazines are reporting the wonderful things hypnosis can do. Hypnotism today is proving that a power exits within each person, call it mind-power, the power of positive thinking, anything you like. The utilization of this inner force or power enables people to endure pain.

For example, hypnosis has been used successfully in helping alleviate the pain associated with terminal cancer. *Life* magazine in the January, 1954, issue published an article to this effect entitled "The Use of Hypnosis in the Case of the Cancer Patient." Hypnosis and self-hypnosis can also be used to break undesirable habits, develop self-confidence, overcome fear and accomplish many other things which will be described in subsequent chapters. Hypnosis and self-hypnosis operate on the principle that WHAT THE MIND CAUSES, THE MIND CAN CURE. Results vary depending on the susceptibility of each individual to suggestion. Everyone can develop into a good subject with sufficient motivation and practice.

Dr. Milton V. Kline, Research Director for Hypnosis at Long Island University, believes that the usefulness and value of hypnotism "are as infinite as the capacities of the human mind of which it is a function."

As a practical force for good, hypnosis has tremendous potentialities.

Incidentally, hypnosis has been adopted by the Council on Mental Health of the American Medical Association. Many physicians today are using it as an acceptable technique for the treatment of certain specific health problems. Hypnosis has also been adopted by the British Medical Association.

Self-hypnosis in particular is an excellent short-cut to self-improvement. It enables us to acquire a new way of successful thinking and living.

Self-hypnosis works automatically

We like to compare autohypnosis to a laundromat machine. The housewife puts her clothes in the machine, drops the coin in the slot and the machine does the rest while she sits comfortably in a chair reading a magazine or book.

In self-hypnosis, after you are relaxed and have freed your mind (equivalent to the machine) of your particular problem (your laundry), you then suggest to your subconscious mind (the dropping of the coin into the slot) the right attitude you need to take. You suggest to yourself the idea that after you have analyzed your problem thoroughly while in the hypnotic state, your subconscious mind will do the rest. The posthypnotic suggestions you give yourself will become *positive habit-thinking* and the solution of your problem will automatically emerge from your subconscious mind.

Try to think of your mind as a self-healing mind. When you scratch yourself and bleed, nature forms a scab over the scratch to help stop the bleeding and close the wound as a protection against infection. This takes place automatically. We generally assist nature by wiping the wound with some antiseptic solution and applying a bandage. The mind also attempts to heal a psychological wound (the frustration or disappointment) automatically by reminding us that we can and will survive our misfortunes. But you can assist the mind and expedite the healing by giving your mind positive self-suggestions and thus letting your subconscious mind know what you want it to do for you (the dropping of the coin). The subconscious mind will do the rest *automatically*. Remember we all have *mind-power*. It can do wonders for us if we will only make greater use of it. Make it easier for yourself when you have a problem that's troubling you. Relax while your subconscious mind does the work for you.

10 main points in chapter one

1. Hypnosis represents a dream-like or sleep-like state, produced by the hypnotist in a subject (the person being hypnotized). It can also be self-induced.

2. It represents a voluntary acceptance of a suggestion by a patient or subject while in a hypnotic state.

3. Hypnotism refers to the actual science and art of inducing a state of heightened suggestibility in a subject.

4. The phenomenon of hypnosis operates on the principle that the resultant state increases the subject's susceptibility to suggestion.

5. Hypnosis entails a willingness to be hypnotized, acceptance of suggestion, motivation and confidence in your hypnotist.

6. Hypnosis and sleep are not the same thing.

7. Hypnotic phenomena can be demonstrated in almost everyone.

8. Many of us unknowingly have been applying the principles of self-hypnosis in everyday life.

9. Self-hypnosis is a technique or method of putting oneself into a suggestible state and giving oneself and accepting constructive and helpful suggestions uncritically. The subject is in control at all times, before, during and after the state.

10. Self-hypnosis means self-mastery, a short-cut to self-improvement and successful living.

Chapter Two

The 4-A's method
of self-hypnosis:
a step-by-step plan

▬▬▬▬▬▬▬▬▬▬▬▬▬▬▬▬▬▬▬▬▬▬▬▬▬▬▬▬

▲ You have learned what hypnosis is, what is meant by the "hypnotic state" and have cleared up any misconceptions you may have harbored about hypnosis. You have been told about the many things you can expect to achieve through self-hypnosis, that you can use it as a force for good. You are now ready for step-by-step instructions as to how you can relax and induce the hypnotic state so that you will respond successfully to self-given suggestions for coping with common everyday problems. You will be able to apply the technique of self-hypnosis to specific problems such as getting your emotions under control, losing weight, breaking the smoking or drinking habit (or cutting down, as you prefer), overcoming laziness, learning to concentrate better, eliminating nervous tension and fatigue, becoming less moody and depressed, improving your attitude about yourself and others, getting more out of life or anything else you want to achieve.

This chapter, incidentally, is a very important one since it is the KEY to the entire book. Therefore we recommend that you study it carefully. Read it as many times as you find necessary. Memorize each of the steps carefully and thoroughly.

First, decide what you want self-hypnosis to do for you

It is important to go over in your own mind exactly what it is that you want self-hypnosis to do for you. Be certain that you have a clear understanding of just what you want to accomplish before starting the actual application of self-hypnosis.

We have found that the understanding of the problem at the descriptive or conscious level is a prerequisite to a deeper understanding of the problem at the subconscious or non-critical level.

Why not make a list of those personality liabilities you wish to get rid of? Ask yourself: "What are my shortcomings? What problems do I have?" You can do this by writing down questions you wish to ask yourself and making a study of your answers. The following is a sample questionnaire.

1. Do I have an inferiority complex?
2. Do I have a distorted sense of values?
3. Am I overweight?
4. Am I difficult to get along with?
5. Am I too jealous?
6. Do I smoke too much?
7. Do I want to give up smoking completely or cut down?
8. Do I manage money wisely?
9. Do I suffer from excessive shyness?
10. Do most people like me?
11. Am I a health-hypochondriac?
12. Do I dislike myself?
13. Do I seem to have excessive fears?
14. Am I inclined to be sarcastic?
15. What is my major personality handicap?

As we have said before these are only sample questions. You can make the list of questions as long as you wish.

The 4-A's method of self-hypnosis

The technique of self-hypnosis consists of four steps:

1. Autorelaxation.
2. Autosuggestion.
3. Autoanalysis.
4. Autotherapy.

Step 1. Autorelaxation

To induce the state of hypnotic self-relaxation follow these instructions carefully:

1. Select a place or room in your home where you can be reasonably sure that you will not be distracted by the telephone or other unnecessary noises or interruptions. It will help to draw the blinds or subdue the lights. We have found from experience also that soft music often puts our patients more quickly into a state of hypnotic relaxation. You may want to experiment by selecting a type of music that is soothing and conducive to "sleep-like" relaxation.

2. Lie down on a bed or comfortable couch or semi-reclining chair, placing your feet on a hassock or some other firm object serving the same purpose. Loosen all tight clothes.

3. Take three deep breaths. Breathe deeply and slowly.

4. Close your eyes.

5. Say to yourself:

> I am going to relax all the muscles of my body . . . starting from my head to my feet . . . The muscles of my face and neck are relaxing . . . The muscles of my shoulders and chest are relaxed . . . I'm beginning to feel free of all muscle tension . . . My arms feel limp and relaxed . . . The muscles of my thighs, legs and feet are relaxed . . . As I breathe deeply and slowly my entire body is completely relaxed. I feel calm and relaxed all over.

6. During this state of self-relaxation remind yourself that relaxation is a *state of mind*. It means "letting go," relief from anxiety and tension, freedom from excessive fear and worry—thinking pleasant thoughts.

7. Tell yourself also, "Self-relaxation will bring me inestimable health benefits. I am going to devote as much time and effort as I can to practicing the technique of self-relaxation. If I don't succeed in achieving immediate results I am not going to get discouraged. Eventually I will master the art of self-relaxation. Each time I practice it, it will be easier."

The Rapid Method of Autorelaxation. After you have practiced the prescribed method of relaxing yourself each day for more than a week, and you are satisfied that you are able to relax completely, you are ready to use a more rapid method of autorelaxation. This entails the use of a KEY word or phrase such as "Let Go," "Calm Yourself," "Mind Control," "Relax." It can be any word or expression. The important thing is that the word must immediately set into action the process of self-relaxation. You must decide beforehand what you are going to do as soon as you give yourself the particular word-command. It may connote closing your eyes, taking two or three deep breaths, and suggesting that all your muscles from your head to your feet are suddenly becoming limp and relaxed.

We have witnessed numerous demonstrations of persons going into a deep state of relaxation bordering on sleep in a matter of minutes. We know it can be done.

Rapid relaxation can also be achieved in the waking state. You give yourself the chosen word and quickly experience a relaxed feeling throughout your body. Your mind suddenly becomes relaxed and receptive to suggestions. In the hypnotic state you suggest to yourself that hereafter whenever you use the selected word for the specific purpose of relaxing, the relaxation will occur *instantly*. If you are walking, sitting, driving a car, you naturally are going to keep your eyes open. You tell yourself that you are completely aware of your surroundings at all times, and that you are in full control of your mind, except that you are in a state of self-induced relaxation as well as a state of increased receptivity to self-given suggestions. Once you have practiced this rapid method by hypnotically induced relaxation you can congratulate yourself for having achieved your first major step in Self-Mastery. You are ready now to make good use of your subconscious mind by giving it orders, commands, suggestions, whatever you prefer to call them. Your subconscious mind will do for you what you want it to do. By repeating and repeating a given suggestion to your subconscious mind, you will ultimately accomplish your objective, whether it is losing weight, giving up smoking, controlling your temper or overcoming a particular fear or phobia.

Step 2. Autosuggestion

You will recall that hypnosis and self-hypnosis work on the theory of *suggestibility*. Just as we are susceptible to being influenced by others we are also susceptible to being influenced by our own thoughts. *The voluntary acceptance of a suggestion is essential to successful self-hypnosis.*

Through persistent practice you can increase your receptivity to suggestion. A "suggestibility test" is a test to determine your ability to *accept* and be *influenced* by a suggestion, thought or idea either given to you by another person or self-given.

Here are three suggestibility tests you can practice.* For self-hypnosis use whichever test you prefer.

1. *The Eye Closure Test*

Pick out some object above eye level so that there is a slight strain on the eyes and eyelids. It can be some spot on the ceiling. Try to get your eyelids to close at the count of ten. If you experience the irresistible urge to close your eyes on or before

---

* The following three tests have been recommended by Melvin Powers, author of *A Practical Guide to Self-Hypnosis*, and Jack Heise, author of *The Amazing Hypno-Diet*.

you reach the completion of the count, you know that you are
in a state of heightened suggestibility or self-hypnosis. This is the
first test for determining if you have achieved self-hypnosis. Give
yourself more time if you don't succeed at first. You are probably
not relaxed enough.

If your eyes do not close involuntarily, close them voluntarily
and follow through with the desired posthypnotic suggestions
as though you were in the hypnotic state.

Here are suggestions that you can use to accomplish the eye
closure test. Do not memorize the exact words; just the form
is important.

> As I complete the count to ten, my eyelids will become
> very heavy, watery and tired. Even before I complete the
> count of ten, it may become necessary for me to close my
> eyes. The moment I do, I shall fall into a state of self-
> hypnosis. I shall be fully conscious, hear everything and be
> able to direct suggestions to my subconscious mind. One
> . . . my eyelids are becoming very heavy . . . Two . . . My
> eyelids are becoming very watery . . . Three . . . My eyelids
> are becoming very tired . . . Four . . . I can hardly keep my
> eyes open . . . Five . . . I am beginning to close my eyes . . .
> Six . . . My eyelids are closing more and more . . . Seven
> . . . I am completely relaxed and at ease . . . Eight . . . It is
> becoming impossible for me to keep my eyelids open . . .
> Nine . . . My eyes are closed, I am in the self-hypnotic
> state . . . Ten . . . I can give myself whatever posthypnotic
> suggestions I desire.

2. The Swallowing Test

Here is another test you can use to determine if you have
achieved self-hypnosis. You can give yourself this test directly
after your period of relaxation or following the eye closure test.
This test is known as the swallowing test. Here are the suggestions you can use:

> As I count to ten and even before I reach the count of ten,
> I shall get an irresistible urge to swallow one time. As soon

as I swallow one time this feeling will leave me and I'll feel normal again in every respect. One . . . My lips are dry . . . Two . . . My throat is becoming dry . . . Three . . . I am beginning to get an urge to swallow . . . Four . . . This urge is becoming stronger . . . Five . . . My throat feels parched . . . Six . . . The urge to swallow is becoming stronger and stronger . . . Seven . . . I feel an involuntary urge to swallow . . . Eight . . . This involuntary urge is becoming stronger and stronger . . . Nine . . . I must swallow . . . Ten . . . I have swallowed one time and am now in a self-hypnotic state in which I am very receptive to suggestions.

With this test you wait until you swallow without conscious direction. When you do, you know you have achieved a state of heightened suggestibility. The act of swallowing has been directed and controlled by your subconscious mind as ordered by your conscious mind. After the swallowing test is successfully completed you can give yourself whatever suggestions you want to.

3. The Hand Tingling Test

This is a third test you can use for determining your receptivity to suggestions. You use the same general pattern that you did for the eye closure test and swallowing test. Remember, these suggestions should not be memorized verbatim; just the form is important.

As I count to ten and even before I reach the count of ten, I shall experience a tingling, light or numb feeling in my right hand. One . . . I am concentrating upon my right hand . . . As I think of it, picture it . . . completely relaxed . . . Two . . . I shall feel a pleasant . . . tingling . . . sensation . . . in my hand . . . Three . . . In my mind . . . I see my right hand . . . It's limp . . . and heavy . . . very relaxed . . . Four . . . I am completely at ease . . . Five . . . My hand is beginning to tingle . . . Six . . . It's a very pleasant

sensation . . . relaxed . . . tingling . . . Seven . . . It is
becoming stronger and stronger . . . Eight . . . It is a very
pleasant feeling . . . Nine . . . I can feel a very pleasant,
tingling feeling . . . Ten . . . I am now in a state of self-
hypnosis and give myself beneficial posthypnotic suggestions.

If your subconscious mind has taken over, you will find your
right hand has a tingling sensation in it. You must remember
after any test with body action, a direction must be given to
have it return to normal. Otherwise, the light, tingling sensation
could continue after the completion of hypnosis. Now you say:

The sensation in my hand will go away, it will return to
normal . . . I now have proof . . . that I have reached a state
of hypnosis . . . Every muscle . . . and nerve . . . in my entire body . . . is completely relaxed . . . I feel wonderfully
well . . . I shall now give constructive instructions to my
subconscious mind . . .

At this point, you may start giving yourself specific suggestions. These suggestions should be carefully planned in advance
of induction so that you will know what to tell your subconscious mind.

How did you do with these tests? Were you amazed at your
own suggestibility—or did you have just a fair degree of response
to your own suggestions? No matter how much or how little
success you had, remember you can do better. Yes, we mean
just that—success will come. If you practice and have achieved
these tests successfully, you will have experienced the first or
light state of hypnosis. You can now achieve wonderful results
using posthypnotic suggestions. You will begin to experience
the power of your own mind—you will become master of your
own fate. As you practice self-hypnosis and use it as a force for
good, you will see that your own "mind control" can influence
your habits. You will become aware of what Dr. S. J. Van Pelt
refers to as the "Power Within." *

* S. J. Van Pelt, *Hypnotism and the Power Within* (New York: Fawcett
Publications, Inc., 1956).

You have learned the technique of self-relaxation and have tested yourself for suggestibility. As we have said before, the ability to do these things has always been with you—like an unused muscle. Now you are putting this power to work—possibly for the first time. You are just turning on the power switch. You are ready to give yourself suggestions for analyzing and solving some personal problem, breaking a habit, developing a better personality or acquiring a more positive philosophy of life.

Step 3. Autoanalysis

Begin with self-relaxation. Follow this with the eye closure procedure. Then give yourself the suggestion that you now are ready to solve your specific problem. Analyze every aspect of it. Regress as far back into the past as is necessary. Try to associate the events and circumstances in your life that led to the development of your particular problem. This kind of soul-searching comes under the category of *hypnotic self-analysis*. The term is self-explanatory. It refers to analyzing and understanding yourself while in a self-induced hypnotic state. It is valuable from the standpoint that you will become enlightened with the answers to many questions you would like to ask yourself, such questions as:

What kind of a person am I?
How is my health affected by the way I think?
To what extent am I oversensitive?
Do I really want to improve?
What plans have I made for the future?
Am I inclined to blame my parents and others for my deficiencies?
What is my attitude concerning sex, love, marriage?

You will be amazed how much you will learn about yourself. This method will enable you to realize your faults so that it will be easier for you to correct them. Take one or two questions at a time, and try to think of as many possible answers as you can. When you awaken yourself from your self-hypnotic state, write down the answers in a notebook. Study carefully what you have written and try to arrive at some conclusions as to why you think and behave as you do. Remember that *self-knowledge is the key to successful self-discipline.*

Keep two separate sections in your notebook—one labeled "What I have learned about myself" and the other "What steps I have taken to improve myself." You will find that your mind will soon become conditioned to self-improvement. The good results will encourage you to continue the process. You will begin to notice that you are developing *a new set of thinking habits.*

Step 4. Autotherapy

Self-therapy consists of conditioning your mind to positive thinking and a positive plan of action through the use of post-hypnotic suggestions.

We are unable at this point to give specific instructions regarding what to tell yourself or what to do since this depends upon the specific goal you are trying to achieve or the specific problem you are attempting to solve. In other words, the details of this fourth step of self-hypnosis are actually included in the subsequent chapters of the book. For example, you will be given posthypnotic therapeutic suggestions for various habit-breaking problems such as excessive eating, excessive smoking, excessive drinking. You will notice also in those chapters dealing with nervous tension, depression, fears and personality development, you have access to a list of posthypnotic suggestions you can follow or which can serve as a guide to help you formulate your own autotherapeutic instructions.

By self-therapy, we infer hypnotic self-therapy. It is based on the principle of "I can—I must—I will—achieve my goal—that I have the mind-power to accept and carry out certain self-given suggestions which will enable me to overcome almost any handicap, to improve my personality and acquire a healthier philosophy of life."

How to achieve
self-hypnosis in the waking state

Self-hypnosis in the waking state can be accomplished by going through the routine of self-induced relaxation, eye closure and then opening your eyes, reminding yourself that you are still in a hypnotic state. You are now ready to give yourself audibly or mentally whatever *constructive* suggestions you wish to put into practice.

How to rouse yourself
out of the hypnotic state

After you have completed giving yourself posthypnotic suggestion, either in the sleep-like or waking state, you can tell yourself that at the slow count of ten, you will rouse yourself from the self-hypnotic state with a feeling of emotional *well-being,* inspired by the conviction that you are going to benefit immensely from the application of the particular suggestions you have given yourself.

Always keep this in mind

Incidentally, should you have any apprehension about self-hypnosis in the event of an emergency, let us reassure you that you will not lapse into a state of unconsciousness—that you will always be aware of everything that is happening at the time and will always be in control of any unexpected situation that may arise.

For example, should any unforeseen circumstance occur, let us say you smell smoke from a fire, or someone calls you for help, you would always be able to interrupt the hypnotic state automatically and immediately respond to the given emergency situation. It should be comforting to know that your instinct of self-preservation prevails at all times during self-hypnosis.

A word of caution

It would be very unwise indeed if a sick person tried to treat himself with self-hypnosis, not knowing the nature of his illness or the cause of his symptoms. We recommend therefore that you contact your physician first and let him decide if the pain in your abdomen is caused by appendicitis or tension, or if your headache is a symptom of an organic condition, or if your cough is the result of excessive smoking, bronchitis, tuberculosis or some other condition. We assume that no intelligent person is going to depend on a home medical adviser or any similar book for the treatment of a condition serious enough to require the services of a physician. Consequently, it would be prudent to see your doctor first. Let him assume the responsibility of making a correct diagnosis. After he has properly prescribed, he will also advise you if you would benefit from additional help with hypnosis. Under the supervision of your doctor you will be able to become a more cooperative patient with self-hypnosis. You will be less afraid. You will be able to increase your tolerance quotient to pain or discomfort and manage your health complaints in a more mature manner.

Regarding emotional problems

Similarily, one must exercise intelligent judgment in evaluating his own emotional problems. We know that there are minor conditions that an average person can handle by using a home remedy, such as putting iodine on a cut, applying first-aid knowledge for a minor injury or taking aspirin for a mild headache. This also applies to certain emotional problems. For example, not every married couple experiencing domestic difficulty consults a marriage counselor. There are many individuals who suffer from an inferiority complex who do not consult a psychiatrist. Self-hypnosis is not a *cure-all*. You must use discretion and seek competent advice if you are in doubt about the nature of an emotional ailment.

An added advantage: the experience of being hypnotized

Many physicians, psychiatrists, dentists and psychologists who are using hypnosis and achieving successful results with their patients have not only taken courses in hypnotism, given by various teaching groups throughout the country, but have also had the personal experience of being hypnotized themselves. Only in this way were they able to appreciate and prove to themselves what hypnosis can really do. When a doctor has been taught how to induce his own hypnotic state, he is better able to teach his patients the technique of self-hypnosis.

We feel that the best way that you can master the art of self-hypnosis is to undergo the experience of being hypnotized by some qualified practitioner. If this is not possible the instructions in this book will be of assistance to you in learning self-hypnosis and utilizing this state for better emotional and physical health. Having attended several of these courses, the authors were amazed at the large number of professional people who asked to be hypnotized so they could learn the technique of self-hypnosis and how to apply it to some problem of their own.

For example, one physician volunteered as a subject before the class and was taught how he could practice self-hypnosis at home in order to conquer his problem of obesity successfully. He also planned to use hypnotic techniques in his medical practice—helping patients with their problems.

It is logical that the salesman who is convinced of the usefulness of his product is better able to convince others of the value of the same product. Perhaps this is one reason why psychiatrists are required to be psychoanalyzed themselves as a prerequisite for analyzing others. Hence, if you want to put hypnosis to the test, we suggest that you undergo the experience of being hypnotized yourself. It should convince you once and for all about the wonderful things hypnosis and autohypnosis can do for you.

Should you decide to avail yourself of this added advantage, it is recommended that you contact the secretary of the local medical society in your city or county for the names of physicians or psychologists who employ hypnosis. You can also contact the chairman of the psychology department of a local college or university. You may write to any of the following (listed alphabetically):

1. William J. Bryan, M.D.
   American Institute of Hypnosis
   8295 Sunset Boulevard,
   Los Angeles 46, California.

2. Dave Elman
   56 Edgewood Avenue,
   Clifton, New Jersey.

3. Milton H. Erickson, M.D.
   32 West Cypress Avenue,
   Phoenix 3, Arizona.

4. Leslie M. LeCron
   Hypnosis Symposiums
   1250 Glendon Avenue,
   Los Angeles, California.

5. Melvin Powers
   8721 Sunset Boulevard,
   Hollywood, California.

As previously mentioned, most of these lecturers have conducted courses throughout the country, and they can refer you to a practitioner in or near your community who is qualified in the use of hypnosis.

Chapter highlights

1. Repeat to yourself over and over again that *what the mind causes the mind can cure* and that you can *prevent* emotionally induced illness using the techniques of self-hypnosis.

2. Suggest to yourself *daily* that you are capable of helping yourself with self-hypnosis, of solving your everyday problems.

3. Self-evaluation through autoanalysis or self-analysis is the first step toward emotional well-being and well-balanced living.

4. The effort you expend in achieving self-understanding will be well rewarded. Your understanding of some of the root-causes of your fears and anxieties will help in overcoming your problem.

5. Use the introspection you acquire through self-analysis to *benefit* you, not harm you. Don't misuse your insight by letting it depress you. Instead, let it improve your thinking about *everything*.

6. Convince yourself that it takes more than multicolored pills to cure yourself of emotional ills. It requires the intelligent application of *self-knowledge* and the repeated practice of *self-discipline*.

7. Never doubt the fact that you *can change* and improve yourself with self-hypnosis.

8. The benefits from self-hypnosis need not be temporary. You can give yourself as many self-hypnotic or reinforced sessions as you need, and as often as you need them.

Chapter Three

How to communicate with
your subconscious mind

●●

**Self-hypnosis can release
hidden potentials within you**

▲ Why not explore and capitalize on your
hidden assets? Self-hypnosis can make you aware of your abilities and capacities. It gives you the incentive to achieve, to discover for yourself those goals that are attainable.

That self-hypnosis has been used successfully by many people for the achievement of self-mastery is evidenced in the following statment by Melvin Powers, author of numerous books on hypnosis:

> I receive mail constantly from readers of several of my other
> books on hypnosis telling me how they were able to achieve
> certain goals that they never dreamed possible. They write
> that they have achieved self-confidence and complete self-
> mastery and have been able to overcome problems that
> have plagued them for many years. These problems not
> only include strictly psychological troubles but many psy-
> chosomatic symptoms as well. Many have remarked at the
> ease in which they were able to achieve self-hypnosis and

the results they wanted. For them it was as simple as following a do-it-yourself book.

Start by learning to plan your time and energy wisely

The next time you practice self-hypnosis, resolve that you are going to get into the habit of making a list of things to be done each day. It is far better to work out a daily agenda than not to make plans at all. Know *what* you are going to accomplish today, tomorrow and the next day. Ask yourself: "What have I achieved today?" Go to bed with a feeling of satisfaction—knowing that each item on your agenda is now accomplished. Don't put things off, thinking that you will eventually get around to them. Do them *now.*

To become successful give yourself a posthypnotic suggestion that you are going to utilize your time intelligently—that you are going to devote a part of each day to this business of self-improvement, learning, developing some talent, doing something for someone else. Repeat to yourself while in a hypnotic trance that accomplishments are achieved through planning, doing, and the determination to succeed. A *sense of accomplishment gives you a sense of self-confidence.* Self-confidence leads to happiness and success. You tell yourself that you are going to make plans for each new day. You will soon be getting more out of yourself and more out of life. Using the techniques of self-hypnosis you will soon become more *productive.*

When a housewife goes shopping for groceries she finds it easier if she makes a list of the things she needs. It would be unintelligent if she found that every time she forgot an important item she had to inconvenience herself by running back to the grocery store. Your mind wants to know what you expect it to do from day to day. Laborers are told by their foreman what they are supposed to do by a certain time or date. Can you imagine a skyscraper being built without plans, without anyone knowing the details of his particular job or assignment?

Get yourself a pocket notebook. Practice writing down your plans for the day—for the week—for the month—for the year— the next and the next. It gives you *goal-direction*. We need to know where we are going—what we want out of life.

You might ask, "What if every time I make plans something happens with the result that they never materialize?" The answer is to keep on making *new* plans to fit the changed situation.

The magic formula for success is *organized planning*. If you don't believe this, try living differently from the way you have been. Don't become a victim of chance. Influence Fate. Control Fate. How? By making plans—more plans and more plans. Use self-hypnosis to remind you to make plans for each day of your life.

The advantages of intelligent planning

1. *Planning builds self-confidence.* You know beforehand what you are going to do each day. It enables you to develop self-discipline so essential to success.

2. *Planning prevents mind-idleness.* When the brain is idle, it invites mischievous thinking and trouble. As you know, an idle mind is the devil's workshop. Keeping busy with things to be done means being happy with yourself.

3. *Planning gives you direction in life.* You must know where you're going, the goals you wish to attain and how *not* to dissipate your time. As your plans materialize you become inspired by a sense of achievement.

4. *Planning enables you to get more fun out of life.* The habit of day-to-day planning should include time for the enjoyment of life whether it is reading an interesting book, listening to soothing music, playing golf or other sports, seeing a good movie or play or anything else that will relax your mind. To be happy you must make plans for happier living.

Your subconscious mind

The subconscious mind is that part of your thinking that is governed by your *instincts*. Behind all behavior are hidden motivations.

You may have said to yourself at one time or another, "Whatever made me do that? I knew better," or "I can't understand why I used such bad judgment!"

Many of our destructive or primitive impulses arise out of our subconscious mind—fear, anger, jealousy—the impulse to hurt someone, to lie and steal. We often give free expression to them only because we have never learned how the subconscious mind operates in our daily life and consequently many of us have never learned to control these trouble-making impulses. *Self-hypnosis can now teach you how to manage those behavior reactions stemming from your subconscious.*

The subconscious mind takes its orders from our self-preservation instinct, which explains why so many of us are selfish, defensive and afraid. We are forever seeking the gratification of physical pleasure.

Chain-smoking, excessive drinking, compulsive overeating and other neurotic habits stem from influences of the subconscious mind. Psychiatrists speak of "unconscious guilt," "repressed desires," "buried resentments," "ambivalence" (love-hate feelings) which quite often play an all-important role in our daily life.

For self-hypnosis to be successful it is essential to know a bit about this part of the human mind. As Herbert Spencer, the philosopher, once said: "It is the mind that maketh good or ill, that maketh wretched or happy, rich or poor."

When you employ self-hypnosis you are contacting your subconscious mind. Through autoanalysis, as described in Chapter Two, you can explore how your instincts influence your everyday thinking.

Communicating with
your subconscious mind

After you have induced the hypnotic state and feel completely relaxed, talk to your subconscious mind as if you were carrying on a conversation with another person.

For example, you might say something like:

1. You are improving every day.
2. You are becoming more mature every day.
3. You are going to follow the self-suggestions which you implant in your subconscious mind.
4. You are going to use self-hypnosis to develop the personality qualities you desire and also eradicate personality traits which you consider undesirable.
5. You are going to look forward to practicing self-hypnosis and autosuggestion every day at a specific time.

Study your dreams—they can
tell you much about your subconscious self

There is an advantage in trying to recall your dreams. They will tell you much about yourself. In analyzing your dreams you are better able to appreciate those *subconscious* factors which may be disturbing your life and causing you to be unhappy. Once you learn what's causing your unhappiness you will be more successful helping yourself with self-hypnosis.

A series of so-called "bad dreams" in which you commit anti-social acts signifies that you have destructive tendencies. It is necessary to be on guard against habitual negative thinking, particularly if it is directed against individuals. Sooner or later, bitterness against society, hatred of those around us, unbridled sexual or criminal fantasies engender shame and self-hatred. These, in turn, cause emotional illness.

If you find yourself engaging in too many dreams of your

earlier years, it probably indicates that you are retreating too much into the past. It will repay you far more to be concerned with the *present* and the *future*. The past is so much water over the dam. You cannot relive yesterday; what counts is what you do today, tomorrow and the next tomorrow. As Dr. Camilla M. Anderson stresses in her book, *Beyond Freud,** "When a person is in emotional bondage to his past, he cannot experience 'the good life'."

A dream that keeps repeating itself over the years suggests a "root-conflict." Such a conflict can color your entire personality. A person who keeps dreaming of associating with famous people or discovering the cure for insanity or cancer or of acquiring great wealth is overcompensating for a deep-seated inferiority complex.

There are people who dream constantly of falling. The repeated dream of falling may represent a temptation to go astray. It suggests yielding to your impulses. Repeated dreams in which you find yourself in a dangerous or frustrating situation suggests anxiety and fear. They may be the result of actual experiences in your past when life was threatened either by serious illness or an accident. Soldiers often experience "battle dreams" years after the war is over. These are also referred to as "echo dreams."

To remember your dreams you must go to bed with the intention of dreaming. As you fall asleep, let your mind wander. Have a piece of paper and a pencil handy on the bedside table. If, in the middle of the night, or early morning, you are awakened by your dream, turn on the light and jot it down. Then go back to sleep again.

If you dream during the night, ask yourself before getting out of bed in the morning, "What did I dream about?" It is within those first five minutes of awakening that you are most apt to remember your dream. If you fail the first few times, keep on trying. We can assure you that you will finally begin to recall

* Camilla M. Anderson, M.D., *Beyond Freud, A Creative Approach to Mental Health* (Harper & Bros., 1957).

them. Keep this up until you have collected a series of 25 to 50 written dreams. Read them over, study them carefully, and try to evaluate them in terms of what you are about to learn concerning the interpretation of your dreams.

Treat each dream as if it were a jigsaw puzzle. When you have put together enough of these pieces, the picture will emerge. That picture may open your eyes to a new estimate of yourself—a new light on weakness in yourself that your conscious mind has been glossing over—a new light on a vague feeling of unhappiness or guilt haunting you.

How to make your subconscious mind work for you

Your subconscious mind is equivalent to land that is valuable. Man discovered that by drilling for oil he was able to take from the earth a priceless commodity that has been useful for many purposes. There are equivalent *treasures* to be found in your subconscious mind. It only takes a bit of mental digging or exploring plus knowledge regarding how to make your subconscious mind work for you.

If you have a problem, for instance, that's worrying you, or if you have some important decision, go to bed with the idea firmly planted in your mind that you are going to devote a small part of your sleep-time to studying and analyzing your problem, resorting to the technique of hypnotic-autoanalysis, which you learned about in Chapter Two. Will this cause you to have a sleepless night? Not necessarily. Decide beforehand that you are going to devote *only* the first half or full hour of sleep to your problem. After you have found the answer, *suggest* to yourself while still in a semi-sleep state, that you are going to sleep soundly with the satisfaction that you have found the solution. You will experience a feeling of satisfaction for having made up your mind about whatever bothered you. You can utilize sleep-thinking, sleep-concentration for advantage. Your subconscious mind can give your intellect the power to triumph over your emotions. It will enable you to do wiser thinking.

The next time you are confronted with a serious problem, try sleeping on it. Give your subconscious mind a chance to analyze it but be sure to remain hypnotically relaxed all during the time you are trying to arrive at a decision.

▲ *A Major Frustration That Was Converted into an Asset Through Self-Hypnosis.**

I'm firmly convinced that when something undesirable happens or I encounter a disappointment or make a mistake in a decision, I can always reap an advantage of some kind from the experience. I no longer react to frustration as I did at one time, for I know that I can profit from whatever happens, good or bad, in one way or another. Let me cite an example—something that occurred in connection with the writing of this book.

My wife and I decided to take an extensive Mediterranean cruise on the *Caronia* with our two sons, during which time I would have an opportunity to do some writing toward the first draft of this book. I had written other books on previous trips and looked forward to another work-recreation vacation.

In packing, I placed all the reference-material I needed (notes, table of contents, two completed chapters, books and case-illustration data) into a leather briefcase. The day prior to our departure I drove to the pier to leave our luggage. The baggage master suggested that I leave everything with him but my briefcase, advising me to carry it with me aboard ship the following day. In this way there would be no chance of it getting lost, particularly after my telling him about my concern over the value, or rather, importance of its contents to me. As a result I put it back in the trunk of my car, deciding to do as he had suggested. By now you must suspect what happened.

We were out at sea, the baggage had been brought to

* A personal experience as related by one of the co-authors (Dr. C.).

our stateroom. But what about the briefcase? It gave me a cold chill to think that I had forgotten to take it out of the trunk of the car the next day, and that the car had been left behind at my sister's home in New Jersey for the duration of the trip.

My immediate reaction was one of irreconcilable frustration. I felt that I had ruined my trip, in a way—that I would be very unhappy not being able to spend a part of each day working on the manuscript. It soon occurred to me that if I maintained this attitude of frustration throughout the trip, letting it depress me, it would not only be unfair to my wife and sons, but I would be making matters worse by failing to enjoy myself—the primary purpose of taking any vacation. I tried to rationalize that subconsciously I must have wanted to forget the briefcase in order to have an excuse to really relax and have a good time. But as a psychiatrist I was aware of the fact that I was merely playing games with my subconscious. Rationalizing wasn't the answer. Finally, in my sleep, the idea occurred —why can't you still work on the book? Here is a wonderful opportunity to apply self-hypnosis. Through self-hypnosis you can recall the Table of Contents, which you can use as a guide, and you will also be able to write every day as much as you desire since the source of most of your material is in your mind. You may have forgotten the briefcase and your notes, but you haven't left your head or your mind behind.

It would also be a further challenge to write without being able to refer to notes—I would be forced to rely on new ideas for what might be called creative or inspired writing. When I awakened in the morning, my wife remarked about my sudden change in mood and wanted me to account for my cheerful disposition. I decided to find a spot on the ship where I wouldn't be disturbed. As I sat in my deck chair, eyes closed, facing the warm sun, I induced a trance state by relaxing and suggesting quietly to myself that I would remember the Table of Contents with all the sub-chapter captions and that when I awakened myself from the trance state I would write down everything I re-called, including some of the ideas I had jotted down a month or more ago. I told myself it *would* work, it *can* work, it *has* to work—that I haven't forgotten anything—that everything was coming back to me. This was the beginning. I now had the Table of Contents. The following day as we left Madeira for Casablanca, the ocean as calm as a lake, I went back to the same deck chair. Fellow passengers concluded I was taking a brief nap. Little did they realize that I was going into another of my self-hypnotic sessions.

Well, there isn't much more to relate except to say that self-hypnosis had enabled me to write more than I had ever anticipated.

What was originally a frustration that threatened the recreational-happiness of my trip was no longer a terrible misfortune, a handicap. It was instead an *asset*, like a frown that inspires a smile. I had also conquered my subconscious which perhaps was responsible for my forgetting the brief-case in the first place. It was another instance of the power of one's mind—what self-hypnosis can do in time of a sit-uational-frustration.

Self-hypnosis can increase
your powers of concentration

The ability to concentrate is something you can *develop* and cultivate—something you can *learn*. Many of us handicap ourselves by harboring the fallacy that we simply are unable to concentrate. We believe, erroneously of course, that our diffi-culty in concentrating is due to something we cannot explain. We rationalize and tell ourselves that some people are just nat-urally gifted that way as if they were endowed at birth with special powers of concentration.

If you wish to be convinced that concentration is a talent or an asset which anyone can acquire, that there are specific techniques by which you can develop your powers of concentration, we recommend that you read A *Practical Guide to Better Concentration* by Robert Starrett and Melvin Powers.

In the foreword of their recently published book, the authors make the following significant statements:

> It is no secret that knowledge cannot be obtained without concentration, yet millions of people blandly acknowledge they lack this prerequisite to learning. The expressions, "I just can't seem to concentrate" or "I never could concentrate" are so common they occasion very little comment. Indeed, many of those using these rationalizations sound as though they took a measure of pride in their deficiency. The implication of those who say they cannot concentrate is that they are suffering from a congenital condition beyond their control.
>
> Nothing could be further from the truth. Anyone with normal intelligence, and that includes most of us, can learn to concentrate. But learning to concentrate must be preceded by intense intellectual curiosity, a burning desire to learn something about everything under the sun . . .
>
> Increasing your powers of concentration will do far more than help you in the accumulation of abstract ideas and the attainment of a higher cultural level. You will find that concentration leads to logical thought processes which will allow you to solve the daily problems that are causing you stress and anxiety.

You have been taught that self-hypnosis is a technique, a psychological tool for achieving self-discipline, self-relaxation, self-improvement. This is accomplished by means of self-suggestion during the trance or hypnotic state, the state of complete relaxation. If you wish to increase your powers of concentration, repeat the following self-directed suggestions during your sessions of self-hypnosis:

1. I believe I can concentrate.
2. I am going to make concentration a *habit*.

3. I am going to reduce distractions to a minimum whenever I am reading or studying.

4. I am going to visualize myself as a person having a good mind, as having the capacity to listen well, to learn, to become interested in everything, to concentrate better and achieve success in life.

Starrett and Powers believe that this kind of positive self-image and thinking is essential if you wish to improve your concentration powers. They say, "You must first imagine yourself being successful in all your endeavors before the goal can be attained. It is a well-known fact that if we think of something long enough and hard enough, it will tend to realize itself."

▲ *How Self-Hypnosis Enabled Norman to Become a Better Student.* Here is Norman's own account of what he was able to accomplish with self-hypnosis.

> My grades in school were poor because I was unable to concentrate. I was constantly looking off into space and daydreaming about one thing or another. I worried about my grades.
>
> I told Mr. Berger about my problem and he recommended that I try hypnosis.
>
> I learned how to relax and practiced what I had been taught. For example, I would make myself comfortable by removing my shoes and loosening my shirt collar. I then let myself go limp. I told myself I could feel the muscles of my eyes getting tired and that I would soon close my eyes. I felt the relaxation travel from my eyes down my arms and legs until I felt completely relaxed. I told myself that I would also relax my mind as well as my body. I made myself think of something pleasant and remained in this state for 15 to 30 minutes. I then gave myself the suggestion that I would be able to concentrate better and improve my study habits. I counted to 10 and opened my eyes suggesting that I would feel confident and would overcome my fear of taking tests, that I would be able to

remember what I had studied and would get better grades. I gave myself this suggestion daily for many weeks.

My grades have improved, probably because I am able to relax for the first time before and during examinations. When I am relaxed I find that I am better able to think. I have also used hypnosis to help me with other problems.

▲ *Self-Hypnosis Changed Barbara's Life—Helped Her Achieve Greater Success.* While we appreciate Barbara's flattering indebtedness to us for helping her achieve success as an author, we feel she is the one that should be congratulated, for it was her determination and faith in self-hypnosis that accounted for her "dream-success" becoming a happy reality.

Barbara had always wanted to write a book. She "dreamed" about it. However she found herself "mentally blocked," as she put it, whenever she made an attempt to get started.

Despite the fact that she had experience as a newspaper reporter, she was unable to convince herself that she had the ability to write her first book.

After measuring the techniques of self-hypnosis, as described in Chapter Two, she began noticing that she was able to put her thoughts on paper more readily and soon discovered that she had managed to complete a final draft of her book.

We asked her to jot down some of the things she suggested to herself and how she achieved what she had.

I learned to overcome the greatest hurdle of all—the sitting down at the typewriter. I could think of a million reasons why I wasn't ready at the moment to start working.

Using the 4-A's method of self-hypnosis I taught myself to relax. I told myself I was going to discipline myself by awakening at 6:00 every morning and writing two hours before I did another thing. It soon became a habit. I used self-hypnosis to inspire confidence in myself. Before long I realized that I had achieved my goal. I had the satisfaction of having written my first book.

It has been over a year since Barbara came to us, wanting to know how she could use self-hypnosis to attain her one big wish in life.

We are happy to report that Barbara has had two books published, one of which was purchased by a Hollywood producer and will be made into a movie sometime this year.

In one of her recent letters she wrote:

> A wonderful side result of the book-writing is that I now write feature articles and stories instead of straight news and consequently earn more than I did previously at my regular newspaper job.

▲ *Walter's Story: How He Conquered Stuttering with Self-Hypnosis.* Here is how Walter describes what he called his "greatest handicap" in life and what he achieved with techniques of hypnotic self-relaxation and self-suggestion.

> During childhood I was known as the boy who couldn't talk. My stuttering and stammering was so bad I couldn't say two words together. The worst thing that could happen to me was to be asked to stand up in class and give a report. I would try, but I was terrible. My face would turn red and I could hardly get my breath. To say the least, I felt very bad. Girls wouldn't go out with me because of my poor speech. When I graduated my speech improved some but it was still bad and I was always ashamed to speak in front of strangers or more than a few people.
>
> When I first started to use hypnosis I found a new peace. After my first session I was so relaxed that I felt like a new person. The feeling that I had complete rest after the session was wonderful. I taught myself how to use this new technique in all my thinking. I taught myself to think slower, eat slower, and generally bring my life to a slower pace.
>
> After several sessions, my speech was so improved that my friends remarked on how much better I was. This, among other things, gave me the confidence I needed to be able to tell myself, "I will think slower, I will speak slower."

Also, when I found myself getting upset I would think of what I should do, how I could relax. I practiced this at least once a day in the quiet of my office. Then I was able to "take the reins again" with hypnosis.

I have been a SCUBA (self-contained underwater breathing apparatus) diver for quite some years. I find now that I am able to talk to small groups and instead of having the fear of stammering I am so relaxed that I enjoy giving talks and answering questions that are asked. I became President of the Pioneer Skin Diving Club (the club now has 93 trained SCUBA divers) and then President of the Atlantic Skin Diving Council. The council is a group of diving clubs from North Carolina to Delaware.

I have been able to train large classes of up to 80 novices at one time, keeping order and proceeding smoothly during the training program. Together with this I was giving lectures on diving with all its problems.

While I was at one of the President's Cup Boat Races with Coast Guard cutters at each corner of the course, one flipped the driver out after he had slowed down to a speed of 80 miles per hour to make a turn near my diving buddy and me. My buddy and I went in and found him. We kept his head above the water until the cutter could come about and drop the litter to get him. We didn't think he was alive, but we gave him first aid. After coming ashore, the TV station WMAL wanted to interview one of the rescuing divers, so I stepped up without hesitation and appeared on a nationwide TV without one stammering. Before the camera I was perfectly calm and collected. My friends later told how well I had done. The driver of the boat completely recovered after eight weeks in the hospital. This was one of the greatest moments of my life knowing that I may have helped save a life and that I had also conquered my speech defect.

Additional information on speech problems. Anyone wishing additional information in regards to speech problems and what can be done to correct them may write to:

1. The American Speech and Hearing Association
   1001 Connecticut Avenue, N.W.
   Washington 6, D. C.
   They maintain a list of all qualified speech specialists throughout the country.

2. The National Hospital for Speech Disorders, Inc.
   61 Irving Place
   New York 3, New York
   (Founded by the late James Greene, M.D., in 1916)

The following are a few recommended books which should prove helpful to anyone with a speech problem:

1. *Toward Understanding Stuttering*
   By Wendell Johnson, Ph.D.
   Price $.25
   The National Society for Crippled Children and Adults, Inc.
   2023 West Ogden Avenue
   Chicago 12, Illinois

2. *Stuttering and what you can do about it*
   By Wendell Johnson, Ph.D.
   Price $3.95
   University of Minnesota Press
   2037 University Avenue, S.E.
   Minneapolis 14, Minnesota

3. *People in Quandaries*
   By Wendell Johnson, Ph.D.
   Chapter: "The Indians Have No Word for It"
   Harper and Bros.
   49 East 33rd Street
   New York 16, New York
   (This book is available in most public libraries.)

Summary

1. Use the techniques of self-analysis to recall all the important events of your life. Make notes afterward. Study them carefully. Evaluate your present attitudes about everything in terms of these past events and influences. Jot down your conclusions.

2. Try to uncover the hidden motivations behind your various behavior-reactions. Learn to understand your subconscious mind as you were instructed to do. Study your dreams. Get to know your inner YOU.

3. Suggest under a self-induced hypnotic state that you are going to plan everything you do, that you are going to budget your time in a sensible manner.

4. Through self-hypnosis you can make life more enjoyable for yourself. You are entitled to live each day to its fullest.

5. During sessions of self-hypnosis, convince yourself that it is abnormal to remain unhappy, that you can make a successful adjustment to whatever hardships may come your way.

6. Type or print on a card a list of goals and positive attitudes you are going to achieve and adopt. Label them "Daily Reminders." Carry the card with you in your wallet or purse as you would your driver's license, identification or social security card. Refer to it daily. Soon you will be carrying out these printed self-given suggestions until you have them memorized. They can change your entire life from an old to a new and better way of thinking and living.

Chapter Four

The amazing power
of self-hypnosis
for daily health
and weight-control

▲ Everyone desires good health—a sound body and a sound mind. To enjoy better body-mind health you must examine your living habits. Health experts have found that your *modus vivendi* determines your physical and mental well-being.

If you allow yourself to become a slave to habits detrimental to good health, you are going to suffer consequences. We know also that persons who are tense are more apt to indulge in health-dissipations, while those who have learned to relax enjoy better health.

Self-hypnosis is a psychological weapon or technique that can change not only your way of living—it can help you develop what we like to refer to as HEALTH-WISDOM. To achieve health-wisdom you must develop *health-intelligence*.

For example, if you want to give up smoking, lose weight or stop excessive drinking, you can always fall back on the formula of self-hypnosis:

1. Autorelaxation.
2. Autosuggestion.
3. Autoanalysis.
4. Autotherapy.

The important first step is to condition yourself to relax as you were taught. Search out the reason why you have neglected to observe or adhere to sensible health rules. Finally, plan in your mind a course of action which will enable you to enjoy the benefits of better health.

We have outlined for you in this chapter and those following detailed, simple instructions showing how you can use the 4-A's method of self-hypnosis to develop and establish good health-habits and break bad ones.

Establishing good health-habits with self-hypnosis

Remind yourself every morning before breakfast that you are going to make this day a *Good-Health Day*. Become health-conscious. We're not suggesting that you worry over every ache and pain. What we mean is that you watch what you eat, how much you eat, know how many cigarettes you've smoked today, how many drinks you've had, how much sleep you're getting. This kind of daily health-preoccupation has its rewards. A 15-minute self-hypnotic health session every morning will help you control the temptation to overeat, to drink to excess, to work longer hours than necessary.

Daily health reminders

Utilizing the technique of posthypnotic suggestion, repeat to yourself the following:

1. I am going to devote a portion of each day to improving my health.

2. I am going to devote a portion of each day to improving my mind.

3. I am going to engage in some form of moderate daily exercise.

4. I am going to see to it that I go to bed at a regular, reasonable hour so that I get my required rest and sleep.

5. I am going to eat good, wholesome food and not overeat, or overindulge in foods that are not good for my health.

6. I am going to observe common sense rules about cleanliness.

7. If I must smoke, I will smoke in moderation.

8. I will never allow drinking to become a problem; I will use discretion as to how many drinks I have or can handle.

9. I will consult my dentist and physician for a periodic check-up.

10. I am going to take time each day for some form of recreational relaxation to balance my day with work and play.

11. I am going to develop habits that are conducive to making me think better and feel better.

Note: We suggest that you write down the above health-reminders on a small card and read them out loud each morning during a session of waking-hypnosis. In this way you will be conditioning your mind day-by-day to improving your health. Try it.

Self-hypnosis: The modern approach to successful weight-control

A person can definitely reduce to his goal-weight through techniques of self-hypnosis. It is a scientific aid and has increasing acceptance and use by physicians. Because so many people are plagued by doubts about the highly advertised miracle diets, *self-suggestion* is gaining greater recognition as a more desirable means of developing new lifelong sensible eating habits and maintaining weight-control.

Excessive eating is an *acquired habit*. To break any habit successfully, you must understand how the habit developed, and why it exists and persists.

Habits can be disciplined. They can be controlled or broken by the power of self-suggestion.

To cite an illustration of the power of self-suggestion for habit-breaking, here is what the movie actress Connie Stevens (when interviewed by Lydia Lane of *Times Mirror* Syndicate) had to say about "making up your mind" to lose weight:

> When I hear people say that they can't lose weight I feel like telling them what I learned—that as soon as you make up your mind to be thin you can. There are few things in this world that are impossible, and if you are really serious about licking an overweight problem, you can.
>
> I used to cut myself a large slice of cake every time something went wrong. I knew I was going to have to pay for it but there I would sit, stuffing myself just because I was upset. Now when I feel like doing that, I laugh at myself and say, "Oh no, that habit is broken."

All habit-breaking requires patience, stick-to-it-iveness and determination.

The amazing Hypno-Diet

Jack Heise in his book, *The Amazing Hypno-Diet* (New York: Belmont Publications, 1962), a paperback, which we highly recommend you read, claims that "The only way overweight can be controlled is for the patient to form new eating habits." He informs us that thousands of persons have been and are being helped to control overweight with the aid of hypnosis and self-hypnosis and that—

> Teams of medical hypnotists are touring the country conducting symposiums to teach the technique of hypnosis to other physicians so they may offer this aid to patients who

have repeatedly failed in an effort to diet and retain normal weight.

Reports in medical hypnosis journals show almost universal success in assisting overweight persons to not only reach normal weight but to maintain normal weight after they have reduced.

We agree with Jack Heise wholeheartedly that what the professional has been able to do for his overweight patients, we can do for ourselves with the practice of self-hypnosis. The Hypno-Diet is a do-it-yourself project.

Melvin Powers in his book, *A Practical Guide to Self-Hypnosis*, states:

Not all people overeat because of emotional problems. Regardless of the reason for overweight, however, the use of self-hypnosis is one of the best answers to the problem.

Overeating is a form of "psychic suicide"

Overeating in some respects can be regarded as a vicarious form of suicide. Fat people often have a fatal "eat-and-be-merry-for-tomorrow-we-die" philosophy of life. They become indifferent to the health-complication resulting from too much food or too much alcohol.

It is an established fact that obesity shortens your life span. It is a serious and unnecessary health-hazard. Insurance companies and statisticians, for example, report that a person who is overweight and is past middle life is more apt to succumb to premature death from such conditions as coronary thrombosis, diabetes and arteriosclerosis, than a person in the same age group whose weight is average or below average. They also point out that a person with a 20 per cent increase in weight over normal and who is 45 years of age has increased his mortality risk 30 per cent; an increase in weight of 40 per cent over normal in the same person increases the comparative mortality risk of 80 per cent.

Yet despite this risk to one's life, there are approximately 16½ million Americans who are doing nothing about their overweight problem. They continue to "dig their graves with their teeth" so to speak.

Obesity and emotional problems

All doctors know that there exists a definite interrelationship between obesity and emotional maladjustment.

They have observed that patients suffering from an obesity problem are in need of so-called *personality-therapy*. By personality-therapy is meant *insight-therapy*. The person who has the troublesome problem of losing weight needs to uncover the subconscious cause or reason for his *compulsive eating*. He must learn to understand the origin and psychology of his emotional conflicts. A better understanding of himself is a step in the right direction. It results in a better understanding of his overweight problem.

The wife of a patient reported that whenever her husband, who was on a strict diet because of overweight, was emotionally upset, following a quarrel with her, he would walk out of the house to the corner drugstore, treat himself to a double rich malted milk, order a piece of pie à la mode, and wind up with a chocolate bar or candy (a typical illustration of emotional immaturity—an escape from an unhappy situation).

Excessive weight and sexual inadequacy are occasionally related. Some men suffer from what is called "nutritive libido"— a food drive comparable to the sex drive except that they often get more pleasure from frequent and excessive eating than from physical relations with their wives.

Nervous tension also causes many people to eat to excess, to smoke to excess and to drink to excess. Self-suggestion dispels tension. It enables you to achieve a state of self-relaxation. Once you learn to relax, the compulsion to overeat disappears. You discover that your eating orgies as an outlet for tension and frustration become unnecessary.

Calorie counters are all very good and those special diets, magic-food diets, and so forth are scientifically interesting; but not until a person understands the psychological or emotional factor in weight-control can anything healthful and permanent be done.

You can't roll off, squeeze off, or melt off fat. Speed is not always so important as it seems to dieters. Dieting is *mental*.

A nine-step program for weight-reduction

Step 1: Devote the initial session of self-hypnosis to making a *definite decision* about your weight-problem. Get yourself completely relaxed, induce the hypnotic state and begin by admitting to yourself that you *have* a problem (assuming that you are overweight) and that you need to do something about it, beginning *right* now.

Note: There *never* must be any doubt in your mind that you *can* lose weight.

The right mental attitude (an enthusiastic determination to achieve your goal) gets you off to a good start. Remember that mind-power is based on the will to succeed.

Step 2: Give yourself the posthypnotic suggestion that the best way to start is to subject yourself to a complete physical examination by your physician. Let him find out what physical conditions need to be corrected. You may be anemic or suffer from high blood pressure. You may need vitamins. Tell him you want to lose weight. He will help you. Ask him how much weight you should lose each week. This is the intelligent way of losing weight. You cannot go wrong if you are guided by your physician. In this way you have the confidence that you are not overlooking a physical health problem that needs attention.

Step 3: Tell yourself all the reasons why you should reduce—what the medical profession has written about the hazards—the illnesses common to those who are overweight—how insurance companies regard persons who are overweight as poor risks.

Osler, the famous physician, advised every man after 50 to modify his diet, to eat less and to abate his appetite. The average middle-aged person has a tendency to become self-indulgent for delicacies and consumes more food than his body can use.

For an excellent book on the subject of overweight and its relation to hardening of the arteries we recommend that you read *The Low Fat Way to Health and Longer Life* by Lester M. Morrison, M.D. (Englewood Cliffs, N. J.: Prentice-Hall, Inc., 1958).

Step 4: Establish a *proper motivation* for wanting to lose weight. Why is it important that *you* lose weight? Repeat to yourself over and over again all the reasons why you would like to reduce.

Step 5: Analyze your eating habits. Ask yourself: "How often do I eat? What foods do I eat? How much do I eat? Where are most of my excess calories coming from?"

Step 6: Determine the reason you overeat, eat the wrong foods, or indulge in between-meal nibbling. This entails more self-analysis—more self-questioning: "Do I eat to excess because of frustration of some kind?" "Am I unhappy?" "Am I starved for love?" "Is it emotional hunger?" "Am I trying to make food a substitute for something else?" "Am I regressing to childhood when I once ate too much cake, ice cream, and candy?" "Am I overweight because of repressed marital unhappiness?" "Is my obesity caused by feelings of hostility?"

Step 7: To diet successfully, make a list of all foods you can eat and cannot eat. Memorize them. Know all about calories. Know at the end of each day if you exceeded your calorie-intake for that particular day. With the aid of self-hypnosis you can condition your mind through autorelaxation and posthypnotic suggestion that you don't have to eat the wrong foods—that all eating (the kind of food you eat and the amount) is a *habit* and that habits can be controlled or broken by the power of self-hypnotic suggestion.

Step 8: Decide in advance what you are going to eat. Weigh yourself daily. Keep your weight-reducing goal constantly in mind. Become weight-conscious. Keep a weekly progress record. See your weight curve come down. Reward yourself after you have made considerable progress by buying a new dress or a new suit in a smaller size. Take pride in your appearance. You'll find that when your friends comment on how well you look, how different you look, your ego will be where it should be. You'll have no reason to feel inferior or self-conscious because of excess fat.

Step 9: Repeat daily that you can and will maintain your ideal weight, that you have now developed new eating habits, sensible ones and that you are no longer susceptible to temptation, *that your mind is in command at all times—that you can still enjoy good food, eat well and not gain back the weight you have lost.*

▲ *This Nine-Step Weight-Reduction Program Works. Here Is an Illustration.* Dr. X is a practicing physician in his middle fifties, about five feet, five inches tall, happily married and the proud father of two fine boys. He loves good food, foreign wines and exotic desserts and cook-outs with his neighbors. However, when he weighed himself upon returning from a restful vacation, he was surprised to discover that he weighed 197 pounds. Being a physician no one had to tell him that for his age and height this was a potentially dangerous weight. About ten years ago he had what he himself diagnosed as a coronary attack. The electrocardiogram findings were suspicious. Despite warnings from a colleague who was a heart specialist, he continued to eat more than his body required. He made unsuccessful efforts to lose weight. Worried that he might suffer another heart attack he decided that he would stop at the Mayo Clinic while on vacation and get a thorough physical check-up. He was given good news and bad news. The good news was that his heart was in good condition and there was nothing in his electrocardiogram to indicate any coronary condition. The bad news was that he had a diaphragmatic hernia or what they called a "hiatal hernia" and that there was a slight increase above normal in his blood sugar. He was instructed to go on a 1000-calorie-per-day bland diet and lose 37 pounds. It was explained to him that if he didn't lose weight he was inviting complications that would make him a bad surgical risk in the event he had to undergo an emergency operation for a strangulated or ulcerated hernia. All this frightened him, to be sure, but not enough for him to adhere to his diet. He had read quite a great deal of literature about the wonderful results that physicians were getting with hypnosis, especially when applied to cases of obesity. Because he was very self-conscious about his excessive weight, knowing he had helped his patients to reduce but he had not followed his own advice, he made up his mind to seek help through hypnosis. Hypnosis had always fascinated him. He read numerous books on the subject and as a consequence he proved to be a good hypnotic subject. He was very cooperative and receptive. He mastered the technique of self-hypnosis and gave himself a daily 15-minute session. He practiced self-hypnosis in the waking state. He could induce the hypnotic state in a matter of minutes and bring himself out in an equal amount of time. Because of this ability to allow his subconscious to influence his conscious mind he was able to say "no" whenever someone tried to tempt him by offering him a second helping or a dessert that was not included in his diet.

If you were to see him today, minus 37 pounds, you would never believe he was the same person. He committed to memory the nine-step weight-reduction program, and carried out each step. He started with Step 1 by admitting he had a weight problem, that he would always be prone to becoming obese and that he was going to do something about it, not tomorrow but today. He was pleased that he had a thorough physical check-up (Step

2) and that he knew how he stood as far as the findings were concerned. He resolved to return to Mayo's for an annual check-up as he has the highest respect for the Clinic's well-earned reputation.

As for Step 3, he was already aware of the hazards of obesity. After all, he was a physician and had treated numerous patients who developed health complications because of overweight.

He had the *motivation* that is needed to lose weight (Step 4). Loving life as he does, he did not want to deliberately curtail his life span.

In analyzing his eating habits (Steps 5 and 6), he discovered that his compulsive eating was associated with tension, which he built up especially when he saw too many patients. Although he boasted that he never allowed his patients to upset him, subconsciously he experienced inner tension. He tried to counteract the strain of a large practice with pleasurable foods. It was the habit of late snacks, the second martini and the occasional ice cream sundae that did the damage.

He became a calorie expert (Step 7) and became accustomed to avoiding foods he shouldn't have.

In Step 8 he agreed that he would have to weigh himself every day—that it is easier to lose that extra one pound than to battle taking off 10 pounds or 37 as he did originally. He claimed he could never adequately describe how wonderful it felt to look well in a smaller size suit and how less tired he feels after shedding all the excess baggage.

Some people confess that they became depressed after losing quite a bit of weight. Our physician friend experienced the opposite reaction. He developed a feeling of well-being. He took greater pride in his appearance and rewarded himself with an entire new wardrobe. His wife and children frequently comment on how well he looks.

We're sure you'll agree with us that he deserves to be congratulated. It's not what hypnosis did for him. It's what he accomplished through autohypnosis—what he did himself for himself. He realized the wisdom of repeating to himself during his sessions of self-hypnosis "Physician—Heal Thyself."

**What losing weight
the self-hypnosis way will do for you**

1. It will definitely improve your appearance.
2. It will prolong your life.
3. It will keep you from developing health-complications associated with obesity, such as hardening of the arteries, coronary disease, diabetes, etc.
4. It will change your personality by giving you greater self-confidence, a sense of pride, a feeling of accomplishment.
5. It will make you less tired and sluggish.
6. It will make you more popular with the opposite sex.
7. It will give you the inspiration to conquer other challenging problems.
8. It will improve your sex life by making you physically more attractive.
9. It will help you like yourself better.
10. It will enable you to help and encourage others to lose weight by your becoming an example of what you've been able to achieve through your own efforts.

▲ *How Mrs. Winston Used Self-Hypnosis to Conquer Her Weight Problem.* Mrs. Winston had read our article on self-hypnosis which had been published in *The American Weekly*—describing how one can break undesirable habits such as overeating, nail-biting and compulsive drinking. Having tried everything without success she made up her mind that she was going to subject herself to being hypnotized and learn about self-hypnotic methods of weight-control.

We asked her to write for us the story of her struggle to lose weight.

> My problem was one of overweight. All the members of my family have had a tendency to accumulate excess fat

from the age of approximately 28 until they developed some illness, which forced them to diet. I have always been healthy so I did not have the same incentive to lose poundage as my sisters and brother had, but other factors contributed to my desire to lose weight. I was uncomfortable both mentally and physically; my clothes were too tight and I disliked having to buy larger and larger dresses most of which were frumpy looking or expensive. My feet, which, strangely enough, remained the same size, protested the increasing burden I placed upon them by reminding me constantly, through pain, of the load I expected them to support. It was awkward for me to get in or out of cars and once I was in, it was almost impossible for me to shift my position.

Although I tried, sporadically, to lose weight by dieting, I was not able to shed many pounds, so finally, I asked the advice of a doctor. He told me my difficulty was caused by a malfunctioning of my thyroid gland. He prescribed thyroid to speed up my metabolism and dexedrine to help me curb my appetite. In addition, he put me on a low calorie diet. When I followed this program, I would lose weight gradually, only to regain it whenever I stopped taking the medicine.

In 30 years, I went to six doctors in various parts of the country, and they all concurred in the diagnosis and the treatment for my condition. The main trouble was that my system would build up a tolerance for the medicine, and then the doses had to be increased. I kept cutting down on the types of food I ate—fats, sugars, starches— but I found that as I approached a weight that would be right for me to maintain, it became ever more difficult to achieve my goal, and I had to cut down more and more on my intake. Luckily, the medicine had only one harmful effect that was apparent: My jaws ached from being clenched all the time.

During the 30 years of my various up and down cycles, I went up to 196 pounds, down to 160, up to 190, down to

180, up to 186, down to 170, up to 197, down to 160, up to 231, down to 173, and up to 219.

In August, 1959, I had a complete physical examination by an excellent doctor and friend who told me my metabolism was a little high. That meant that no longer could I rely on any medicine to help me lose weight. I felt that now for reasons of health, it was necessary to get down to normal size because the amount of sugar in my blood was slightly above normal. Here I was at 215 pounds and faced with the problem of losing 60 of them without the medicine to assist me.

I had explored various short-cut and fad methods for reducing, but after an initial rapid loss, up would go my weight and appetite. It seemed to me that every friend I had and all the advertisers were in league against me. Even my doctor friend, who had spent much of his time trying to get my weight down, would load my plate with succulent food on holidays. My friends were actually trying to kill me with sweetness by tempting me with delicious meals, candy, alcoholic drinks, and huge pieces of calorie-laden cake. Most social activities include feasting of some kind. It's hard to imagine ball games, circuses or carnivals without hot dogs, pop corn, ice cream, peanuts and other food enemies.

I had heard about the use of hypnosis as a means of strengthening will power. I considered consulting a psychologist to solicit his aid in assisting me to follow a regime of semi-starvation, which I expected to be quite rugged. The main reason I had delayed in seeking such help was because I wanted to be sure the psychologist was a bona fide therapist. I didn't want to get into the clutches of a charlatan.

In the meantime my weight was gradually increasing, and when it reached 219 pounds, I finally phoned and made an appointment with Mr. Joseph R. Berger, the co-author of the article on hypnosis, which I had read.

My first visit to see him took place about the middle of

February and the time was spent in getting acquainted. He asked about my health, and when I assured him that a recent physical examination by a reputable doctor had proved me to be reasonably healthy for my age and weight, he decided to help me, but it wasn't until the next visit on February 22, that he began hypnosis.

I had always assumed that a hypnotist put a patient in a deep trance, during which he made such strong suggestions, and that these suggestions could be followed without much effort. He explained that the subject is not only conscious at all times, but that he must cooperate fully with the hypno-therapist if he expects to get favorable results; that he must put complete faith in the method employed and in his ability to surmount his problems; that he must have confidence in the hypnotist; and that he must control his natural tendency to "resist."

At first the going was rough. I cut down on the number of calories I consumed daily, but I was expecting a miracle, which didn't take place. He told me to follow my doctor's advice in selecting a diet and in everything else that concerned physical health. Although I did not lose much weight at first, I persisted in my efforts. I had decided that I would continue for about six months even if I didn't lose a pound. Meanwhile, he was probing the inner recesses of my subconscious in order to determine the cause of my obesity. He used the positive method of persuasion. He emphasized the pleasant aspects of having a slender figure. At my age, getting a man, wearing a smaller size dress or increasing my popularity-rating did not act as incentives to abstain from high caloric foods. I was more interested in comfort, freedom from pain, and ease of movement.

In my effort to get my weight down, I turned at last to self-analysis in order to discover the reason for my resistance. After a while I began to understand that the cause of my block originated in my childhood.

My parents were strict disciplinarians. All of us, my

brothers and sisters as well as myself, were never cajoled
into doing things. We were expected to follow certain prescribed rules of acceptable behavior. Any transgression
from these rules brought swift and certain punishment. As
a child my reaction to the harshness of this treatment took
the form of overeating. And once this pattern was established it continued into my adult life.

Just before each meal I practice placing myself in a
hypnotic state according to the way I have been taught.
During these pre-meal three- to five-minute sessions, I remind myself of the reasons why I want to lose weight, the
harmful consequences of being fat and the confidence I
have developed of being able to eat sensibly, choosing carefully what I eat and controlling the amount of food I eat.
My self-hypnotic sessions might be compared to the practice of saying grace before each meal. It requires so little
effort and the results have been very encouraging.

I am pleased to say that I have been losing weight
steadily and to date I have lost 50 pounds. My doctor is
pleased with what I have achieved. He found me in better
health than I was before my latest reducing venture. In
fact, my health is perfect. My feet can endure more than
they could last year, and I find it much easier to move
about in small spaces, cars, or buses, for instance. I am
much more interested in wearing jewelry, shopping for
new clothes, trying new hair styles, and in experimenting
with make-up.

I have complete faith in self-hypnosis. I have tried it
and it works. I have given away all my larger clothes. During the former up and down cycles, I used to store the large
dresses to have them handy for the up half of the round.
But now, as soon as I discover that I am putting on weight
I resort to a few self-hypnotic sessions and I quickly come
down to my desired weight.

▲ A *Case of Emotional Hunger.* One of our patients related
that she would sometimes drink a bottle of maple syrup whenever she was depressed and unhappy. She claimed that she was

unable to control her craving for sweets. During her depressed spells she would consume a quart of ice cream or eat a box of chocolates.

As you might surmise, she was 30 pounds overweight. This mania for sweets was a symptom of her *emotional immaturity*. She had a pretty face and was very narcissistic despite her dislike of her obesity. She admitted that during childhood and adolescence she had never been taught self-discipline, was allowed to eat everything and anything, and was given whatever she requested.

As an adult, Lillian had never been able to establish a normal relationship with the opposite sex. She feared marriage and at the same time spoke of being "starved for affection." She craved the same attention from strangers that she had received from her parents. Whenever she met with rejection she withdrew into herself and overindulged in an orgy of pastries and sweets to gratify what might be diagnosed as "emotional hunger."

We taught her techniques of self-hypnosis as outlined in this book. She learned to apply the insight she gained and happily discovered that she could control her craving for sweets. Self-hypnosis also helped her to prevent tension, depression and moodiness, which had acted as opposing factors in her battle to lose weight.

Salient points

1. Self-hypnosis can change your way of living. It can help you develop good health-habits and break bad ones.

2. Compulsive overeating is a form of "mental suicide."

3. Obesity is very often associated with emotional frustration.

4. Put into daily practice the nine-step program for weight-reduction.

5. Remember that you can definitely achieve successful weight-control using self-hypnotic techniques.

Chapter Five

Self-hypnosis,
smoking, and alcohol

▲ Many heavy smokers find it difficult to
stop smoking only because they have never taken the time to
study everything that they need to know about the smoking
habit. They argue that some smokers have lived to an old age—
that there seems to be a difference of opinion among the medical
experts as to whether smoking causes lung cancer. Others feel
that smoking relaxes a person, or that a person who abruptly
gives up smoking will become irritable and difficult to live with,
gain weight or even suffer a nervous breakdown. To this group
also belong those who believe that they "just can't give up
smoking"—that they "don't have the kind of will power it takes."

Facts about smoking

If you harbor any misconceptions about tobacco and its effect on your health, it is naturally going to be more difficult for
you to stop smoking. Consequently we recommend that you
acquaint yourself with the following facts:

1. *Nicotine is a poison.* Although it has a stimulating effect
on the nervous system, it is still classified as a poison. It is pos-

sible to kill an animal with certain concentrated amounts of nicotine. Fortunately the amount present in tobacco has never been enough to prove fatal to human beings.

2. *That smoking is harmful to one's health is an established fact.* Smoke is an irritant to lung tissue and mucous membranes. That is the reason a person often complains of "smarting of the eyes" when in a smoke-filled room. While not all cases of lung cancer can be attributed to tobacco, it is a known fact that many persons who died of lung cancer were heavy smokers.

Athletes are generally forbidden to smoke during their training period. There must be a valid reason for it. A disease known as Buerger's disease, causing needle-like pains in the lower extremities, has been linked to excessive smoking. Some insurance companies, according to their statistics, claim that longevity is curtailed by excessive smoking. Most doctors recommend that patients who suffer from sinus condition, bronchitis, chronic cough, or a heart disease, stop smoking. Again there must be a reason for it. Despite all this evidence more than one billion cigarettes are consumed daily in this country.

3. *Anyone can stop smoking.* Smoking is an *acquired* habit and habits can be conquered. The proof is that many heavy smokers can testify that they were able to give up smoking completely. Psychologists will tell you that breaking any habit isn't a matter of will power. It's more a matter of *unconditioning* and *reconditioning*—substituting one habit for another, developing insight into the reason you are tense and smoke to excess and utilizing whatever techniques prove successful in combating the nicotine-habit. We believe that if you use the techniques of self-hypnosis, you can stop smoking permanently.

4. *Ex-smokers attest to the fact that as a result of giving up smoking they sleep better, no longer suffer from nausea and heartburn, and have whiter teeth; they have no throat irritation, their chronic cough disappeared and they feel less tense.*

5. *Excessive smoking increases nervous tension.* The person who has a compulsion to smoke to excess is generally a tense,

nervous individual. He deludes himself into thinking that smoking relaxes him. Smoking in moderation may have a relaxing effect on some people. But this isn't true if you are a chain-smoker. You become as addicted to nicotine as the dipsomaniac is addicted to alcohol. You have often heard a chain-smoker exclaim, "I'll die if I don't have a cigarette." Heavy smokers are anything but relaxed. Observe a heavy smoker at a cocktail party and you'll find he's inclined to be a "jittery" person. We're not referring to the person who smokes an after-dinner cigar or someone who smokes a half pack of cigarettes a day. The chain-smoker has made nervousness a *habit* and he reaches out for another cigarette as the alcoholic does for another drink. Paradoxically enough, many heavy smokers do not enjoy smoking. They are afraid to stop smoking, thinking they will gain weight. There is no truth in the common belief that if you stop smoking you gain weight. Many heavy smokers have stopped smoking and haven't gained weight.

We contend that non-smokers health-wise are better off than smokers, especially compulsive smokers. If you don't think so, read *How to Stop Smoking* by Herbert Brean (Pocket Books, Inc., 1954).

14 suggestions to follow— if you want to stop smoking

Many of the suggestions mentioned in the nine steps for weight-control also apply to breaking the tobacco habit.

Here are some specific instructions to follow if you wish to stop smoking:

1. During one of your sessions of self-induced relaxation, tell yourself that you have made a *final* decision to stop smoking— and that you are going to start *now*, not tomorrow or the next day and that you aren't going to allow any exceptions—particularly if you *want* to give up smoking altogether.

2. Repeat to yourself daily *why* you wish to stop smoking entirely. Did your doctor tell you to stop smoking? Do you suffer from a chronic cough, pains around the heart or any other condition that makes smoking contraindicated? *The motivational factor is very important in any habit-breaking.*

3. Convince yourself: "Smoking will *never* improve my health. If I need to feel better physically I must be willing to make concessions, and forego certain pleasure-habits that are detrimental to my health."

4. Give yourself the posthypnotic suggestion that you are not going to purchase any more cigarettes and that if you should perchance accept a cigarette you will immediately break it in two as though by compulsion. This will have a tendency to deter you from resuming the smoking habit.

5. Become preoccupied with the thought that the longer you abstain, the easier it will be to give up smoking permanently.

6. Suggest to yourself that you are going to feel proud of yourself—you are going to experience a feeling of well-being and that the conquest of this habit will make it easier for you to conquer other habits harmful to your health.

7. Keep a record of your progress. During each session of self-hypnosis remind yourself that you have abstained successfully so many days, weeks or months, as the case may be. This will tend to encourage you and give you the incentive to continue with your successful self-discipline.

8. Tell yourself over and over again that no habit is stronger than the power of your mind—the same mind that caused the habit to take hold in the first place. It's you versus tobacco. Accept it as a challenge!

9. Never get discouraged or become impatient. Habit-breaking entails patience, perseverance and determination.

10. If you must find a substitute for smoking, try chewing gum or sucking on a Lifesaver or mint. Acquire new and less harmful habits.

11. Suggest away the *desire* to smoke and the habit itself will vanish. Tell yourself, "I really don't enjoy smoking as much as I think I do."

12. If you change your way of thinking and living through self-hypnosis, you will find it easier to change your habits as well.

13. As a non-smoker prove to yourself that you can get as much fun out of life as the habitual smoker.

14. Make a list of all of the advantages of not smoking and refer to it as frequently as you need to.

▲ *Harry Conquers His Addiction to Tobacco With Self-Hypnosis.* Harry consumed from two to three packages of cigarettes daily. He had heard about hypnosis being used to break habits, and he wanted to give up smoking altogether.

His father died at the age of 59 from lung cancer, and the family doctor had expressed the opinion that it may have been caused by excessive smoking. Harry had developed a chronic cough and was experiencing pains in the upper part of his chest. Although X rays of his lungs were negative, he feared he too would someday develop lung cancer.

He wanted to learn all about self-hypnosis. He was quite receptive and we taught Harry the 4-A's method of self-hypnosis described in Chapter Two. He suggested to himself that he would never smoke again nor want to smoke again, and that if he ever attempted to light a cigarette, he would break it in two.

Eighteen months have elapsed and Harry has never smoked since. He claims he has no desire to smoke and feels better physically and mentally knowing that he has been able to conquer a habit that has been worrying him for years.

▲ *The Case of an Attorney Who Gave Up Chain-Smoking Using Techniques of Hypnotic Self-Suggestion.* An attorney who had previously tried to stop smoking many times decided to put what he had just learned about self-hypnosis to the test. He describes his successful triumph over tobacco as follows:

I first began to smoke when I was 17 years old. I have been smoking for the past 38 years. It started with 10 cigarettes a day and gradually increased to a point within the last two years of not being able to do anything without a cigarette or a cigar dangling from the corner of my mouth. I became a chain-smoker. I smoked two to three packages of cigarettes a day, three or four cigars daily and occasionally a pipe. I smoked before breakfast, during meals, between meals and before going to sleep. It began to worry me. It got so bad that I was even talking to people with a cigarette in my mouth.

It wasn't until I began to complain about a chronic cough, sore throat and needle-like pains over my heart that I suspected these symptoms were caused by my excessive smoking. To confirm my suspicions I consulted my doctor who not only recommended that I stop smoking but warned me that my complaints would become worse and that I was risking the development of a serious heart disorder because of excessive nicotine in my system. I knew all the while that smoking wasn't good for me, yet it was difficult to stop. I knew also that I would never be able to smoke in moderation. I had to make a decision. It was either quitting altogether or putting up with my symptoms and risking the consequences.

After many unsuccessful attempts to break the habit I decided to try self-hypnosis. I had read several articles about how self-hypnosis had helped people to lose weight and had helped others who had a drinking problem and I decided that it could help me conquer my tobacco habit.

I subjected myself to being hypnotized and in this way I learned to experience the feeling of relaxation. I concluded that I was using the pressures and problems at the office as excuses for my excessive smoking. I had developed the habit of chronic tension. I was unable to work in a relaxed way. There was no frustration at home in my relationship to my wife or my children, and the only thing that I could attribute my compulsion to smoke to excess was work-tension. I gave myself the posthypnotic suggestions that were recommended and learned to practice and apply the technique of self-hypnosis at home and at the office. I gave myself a session every morning before going to work for about three weeks and found that each day I was learning to enjoy working at the office without the old feeling of tension.

I had stopped smoking completely after my fourth session of self-hypnosis. In subsequent sessions I reinforced the suggestions I had given myself previously and after three weeks I no longer needed to continue using self-hypnosis. My desire for any form of tobacco vanished. My symptoms also disappeared and I have felt better than I have in a long time. I was worried that I would find a substitute outlet in excessive eating, but this has not been the case. In my autosuggestions I told myself that I would not resort to excessive eating to make up for not smoking.

Here are some of the self-suggestions I used to conquer my chain-smoking habit:

I have definitely made up my mind to stop smoking *completely*.

I am not going to fool myself into thinking that I can cut down on smoking or smoke in moderation.

I no longer envy people who smoke.

I am able to say "No thank you" whenever I am offered a cigarette or cigar.

I am going to enjoy better health as a result of giving up smoking.

I am going to feel more confident knowing that I can do almost anything once I have made up my mind.

I no longer desire a cigarette or cigar because I am aware of the detrimental effect tobacco has on my health.

I am convinced that giving up smoking will add years to my life and will eliminate the development of any serious health condition that would curtail my longevity.

I am never going to permit an *exception* by smoking an occasional cigarette or cigar.

I know that I smoked to excess because of tension. Tension only increased my desire for another cigarette or cigar. I was caught in a vicious cycle. Now that I have learned to practice the technique of self-hypnosis, at home and at the office, I will never need to smoke again.

The problem of alcoholism

There are approximately 46,000,000 people who regard themselves as "social drinkers"—over 20,000,000 of them women. The excessive drinkers number around 3,000,000. Of those 750,000 are chronic alcoholics.

The financial loss due to alcoholism is estimated to run around a billion dollars a year.

Subconscious causes of excessive drinking

What you should know about the subconscious causes of excessive drinking before using self-hypnosis: *

There are various theories that help to explain why 3,000,000 people develop a compulsive urge to drink to excess.

Excessive indulgence in alcohol can be traced to a child-mother relationship. The alcoholic is an emotionally immature person with a *nipple-complex*; an adult child who has never been psychologically weaned from his mother's breast—or if bottle-fed, craves a pacifier (alcohol) as a nipple-substitute. Alcohol is actually a fluid-substitute for mother's milk, symbolically speaking. This will seem farfetched if you have never listened to the life stories of alcoholics. If you have, you would learn that most of them "never grew up" and have a strong oral-intake. They regress to the stage, when, as infants, they wanted to put everything in their mouths. The alcoholic, when frustrated, wishes to return to the "nursing" period of his life. Thumb-sucking in the

* F. S. Caprio, *Living in Balance* (N.Y.: Medical Research Press, 1951).

child, then later, weakness for sweets and pastries, chewing gum, smoking, eating and drinking excesses, all are sublimations or hangovers of this same nipple-complex present in all of us.

Those of us, however, who resort to excessive eating, drinking, smoking, suffer from what psychiatrists call *oral erotism* (mouth-pleasures). All alcoholics, in other words, have an *oral-erotic complex*.

Most alcoholics are oversensitive and consequently are unable to withstand the frustrations of life. They are blind to the fact that they are victims of a nipple-complex and hence are unable to discipline themselves sufficiently to give up drinking. Practically all of them, in addition, suffer from an inferiority complex which they try to drown out with alcohol.

The fear of death, tension and separation from loved ones during the war, helped to make soldiers who were oral-erotics more susceptible to wartime drinking.

Another theoretical explanation for excessive drinking is *escapism*.

There are many normal people who dislike getting up in the morning and having to go to work. But such is life. We have to earn our bread; we can't escape our responsibilities.

Flask-carriers want to escape all of life's painful realities. They refuse to admit that through their own efforts and determination they can successfully overcome the normal problems of adult life, though all about them they may see other people doing so.

There are various methods of escaping reality. Some take to gambling, while others become philanderers. Some take "dope" and still others prefer alcohol. The underlying motive, however, is the same, to narcotize or assuage the mental pain caused by personal misfortunes. They apparently anesthetize their unhappiness.

Unpaid debts, an unhappy marriage, failure in business, physical illness, all constitute surface-alibis for excessive drinking. The real truth is that those victims of alcoholism never developed "intestinal fortitude," the deep-seated courage, to endure the common adversities of life.

A third theory is that alcoholism represents a vicarious or *disguised form of self-destruction.*

Many psychiatrists are of the opinion that alcoholics are people who commit what might be termed "psychological suicide." They die a slow death, only because they are unable to recognize the true motive that unconsciously inspires their sense of defeat—their hopelessness. This of course does not apply to the moderate drinker.

Alcohol addiction becomes the compromise between the wish to live and a wish to die. It is a partial suicide—a "poisoning" of the body and mind but usually not enough to cause death. The alcoholic lives and dies at will. He is too scared to die and too afraid to live. *He lives in a third world.*

A fourth explanation why some people drink to excess is for the *release of inhibitions.*

We all have primitive emotions for which we secretly crave an outlet. But we cannot give way to them because our sober conscious mind will not permit.

A man may be too inhibited to show his affection for his sweetheart. From his outward behavior you would assume that he is a "perfect gentleman." But deep inside he wishes he had the courage to put his arms around his girl and profess his love for her. Liquid stimulants loosen his tongue. Alcohol makes him the "Casanova" he wishes to be in real life. He becomes expansive and witty as well as romantic only because he now has an excuse for his bold behavior. If he is rebuffed he can always blame it on that "one cocktail too many."

As Dr. Walter Miles stated: "Alcohol unburdens the individual of his cares and fears, relieves him of his feelings of inferiority and weakness. The inhibitions and self-criticism which ordinarily cramp his feelings tend, after alcohol, to be put aside."

Alcohol releases inhibitions, and temporarily sets the mind free by relieving anxiety. But the alcoholic fails to realize that this is a false personality he assumes. It would be far better for him to dis-inhibit himself through other emotional outlets than to use alcohol as a "crutch."

Use self-hypnosis to help find and remove the cause of excessive drinking

As we have said many times, knowledge is power. If you understand the psychological factors responsible in your particular case for your addiction to alcohol, you have a greater chance of solving your problem.

Here again, like smoking, you must decide whether you want to give up drinking altogether or merely cut down. If you have learned that you have never been able to handle alcohol successfully in any quantity, it may be wiser to abstain completely. This can definitely be accomplished with self-hypnosis.

Use the technique of self-hypnosis to dispel tension. Tension predisposes to excessive drinking. Practice relaxing in everything you do. Walk slower, talk slower, eat slower, think slower. Slowness and relaxation go together. Haste, worry and tension are branches of the same tree.

During sessions of self-analysis trace your habit of drinking to its root-cause in the light of what you just learned about why people drink to excess. Ask yourself a lot of questions. Study your answers when you think you have discovered the subconscious reasons for your drinking, proceed to the final step in self-hypnosis, namely, *self-therapy*.

Give yourself the self-suggestions you need.

The following can serve as a sample of what you should tell yourself. If you wish, make up your own set of posthypnotic suggestions. Repeat them out loud or silently during as many sessions as you may require:

1. I don't have to have a drink whenever I am upset or frustrated. I can survive life's frustrations without alcohol.

2. Because I have proven to myself over and over again that I have never been able to handle alcohol intelligently, I am going to abstain altogether.

3. By giving up alcohol I am going to be rewarded by feeling better physically and mentally.

4. I am not going to depend on someone else to make me stop drinking. I am going to stop of my own accord because I *want* to.

5. Each day that I abstain is a day closer to successful permanent abstinence.

6. I am going to remind myself of the things I have learned and now understand through autoanalysis (the subconscious reasons for my excessive drinking).

7. I am going to find healthier outlets for personal frustrations that arise from day to day.

8. I am going to practice the art of self-hypnosis so that I will never need to depend on *alcohol* to relax me.

9. I am not going to fool myself by thinking I can handle an occasional drink or two.

10. I shall repeat over and over again during sessions of self-hypnosis, "I *must*, I *can* and I *will*—give up drinking entirely."

11. I will avail myself of help from Alcoholics Anonymous if need be. (Alcoholics Anonymous has reclaimed over one quarter of a million alcoholics.)

▲ *Case of Compulsive Drinking That Responded Successfully to Self-Hypnosis.* George was a bachelor architect who worked long hours. He would end his day's work by retreating to his apartment and drinking a pint of whisky every evening. Gradually, this was increased to one or two fifths over the week ends, and he soon found that he was unable to work during the day unless he had a "few drinks." He felt compelled to drink— a beginning symptom of dipsomania (craving for alcohol).

His practice began to deteriorate. He disappointed his clients and developed an indifference toward everything. Nothing seemed to interest him. He withdrew more and more into himself.

Finally he decided he was going to try self-hypnosis. Much to his own amazement, after his third session he stopped drinking. He informs us that now he is able to work without tension and is able to lose himself in his recreational hobby on week ends.

To sum up

1. Tobacco is an irritant to mucous membranes.

2. Many persons who have died of lung cancer were excessive smokers.

3. Chain-smoking is caused by nervous tension.

4. Smoking is a *habit* and as such can be conquered with self-hypnosis.

5. Alcoholism is a *symptom* of a personality maladjustment. It is the symptom-manifestation of some underlying neurosis.

6. The real causes of excessive or habitual drinking are generally subconscious.

7. Disappointments, financial reverses, poor health, grief, unhappiness are secondary or contributing causes and are used as alibis—to cover up some deeper cause.

8. While alcohol in small or moderate quantities lessens anxiety and helps to relax a person, in excessive amounts it acts as a depressant.

9. If you have a drinking problem or you think you are an alcoholic, admit it and begin using self-hypnosis in the same way that you would to break any other habit.

10. Give yourself whatever hypnotic suggestions you need. Repeat them daily.

11. Convince yourself that what the mind causes the mind can cure. If you can *develop* a habit you can also *break* it.

Chapter Six

The hypnotic road
to restful sleep

A common complaint problem

▲ Fifty-two per cent of our population suffer from insomnia. Each year more than a billion sleeping pills are sold.

This should give you some idea of how many people are unable to sleep without having to resort to barbiturates.

Many factors cause sleeplessness

Here are a few of them:

1. *Taking worrisome troubles to bed with you.* You cannot expect to get a good night's sleep if you lie awake worrying about office problems. Whether you're a lawyer, physician, politician, business executive, you must learn to lock your troubles in your desk at the end of each day. At least you should keep them out of the bedroom. It is unfair to your family and surely to yourself. You are entitled to eight hours of sound sleep. You need that much if you expect to live out your normal span of life. If others have trained themselves not to "work in their sleep" then there is no reason why you can't do the same.

2. *Being obsessed with the false idea that you just can't sleep.* Labeling yourself an "insomniac" merely reinforces a *negative suggestion.* You begin to believe it.

This gives you a good excuse to become addicted to sleeping pills. You try different ones. You increase the dosage because you find you have built up a tolerance to the drug. You become afraid to try to sleep without the pills. Soon you start to worry about your sleeping pill addiction which in turn causes more insomnia.

3. *Tension-fatigue.* Going to bed feeling overfatigued may cause you to have a sleepless night. This is because an excess of fatigue toxins tends to stimulate the brain. Many persons have learned that when they went to bed too exhausted, they were unable to fall asleep. As a consequence they relied on a sleeping pill to help bring on sleep. Tension carried over from the day's activities also causes insomnia, particularly if we were subjected to too much excitement or we became involved in some unpleasant emotional episode or argument or experienced an acute frustration or disappointment of some kind. This residual tension causes the mind to become overactive. Like a runner who can't stop himself abruptly at the finish line, he has to keep running until he finally slows down to a walk. The overactive mind keeps working past bedtime, and we find ourselves worrying about something when we should be sleeping.

4. *Pain and discomfort from some illness.* We can hardly expect to sleep well if we are experiencing pain from some arthritic condition, an abscessed tooth, a severe headache. In instances of this kind it is understandable that a person must be given prompt medication by his physician to relieve him of his pain and at the same time promote sleep. Most physicians in treating hospitalized patients realize the importance of prescribing sleeping pills when they are indicated. Your physician should decide for you when you need or don't need something to make you sleep. He assumes you will use good common sense as a protection against becoming addicted to sleeping drugs.

5. *Bad sleeping conditions.* A hard mattress may make sleeping uncomfortable. An infant crying in the night will awaken its parents. Telephone calls past midnight will inevitably disturb one's sleep. Some people are unable to sleep in a strange bed. Others find it impossible to sleep on Pullman trains. If the room is too cold or too warm, it may interfere with sleep. If the husband snores, the wife may find sleeping difficult. Nevertheless, all these factors must be taken into account. Whatever situation or condition prevents one from sleeping well should be remedied.

6. *Sexual incompatibility in marriage.* It would be a serious omission not to include under the causes of insomnia the many husbands and wives who are unable to sleep well because of some sexual problem. Wives who are deprived of sex satisfaction, love and affection are often restless. They become tense and unhappy. Husbands who are rejected by their wives often complain of an inability to sleep. The couple who bicker and quarrel just before going to bed aren't going to enjoy a good night's rest Unhappiness in marriage contributes to insomnia. Happy couples sleep better.

7. *Guilt feelings.* A person who goes to bed with a "bad conscience" may find it difficult to fall asleep. He worries during the night about what he did or said. Some women cry because of guilt feelings, which naturally keeps them awake. Feelings of remorse plague them. Guilt causes fear. Fear brings on anxiety and anxiety results in insomnia. It is not uncommon to hear someone say, "If you don't sleep well, it's because you have a guilty conscience." If your mind is at ease your chances of sleeping soundly are better.

8. *Bad habits.* The person who is disorganized in his living habits is disorganized mentally. He has no routine or schedule to guide him. His eating habits are irregular. He may eat a big meal an hour before going to bed and wonder why he can't sleep. Or he may drink too much and find that he tosses and turns because his mind has been overstimulated by alcohol. He

may go to bed at a different hour each night. Some nights he decides to read up to the early hours of the morning or he may be in the mood to go to bed too early and awaken at 4 A.M. Many people who are unable to sleep turn on the lights and get up out of bed. They may pace the floor and smoke or they go to their refrigerator and eat; others go out for a walk. The next night it's the same thing. You can never cure yourself of insomnia as long as you do things that overstimulate your mind. Turning on the lights and getting out of bed are the wrong things to do. It is far better to remain in bed and learn to relax your mind. We know that self-relaxation is conducive to sleep.

▲ *When Charlotte Learned the Techniques of Self-Hypnosis, She No Longer Needed Sleeping Pills.* Charlotte's insomnia started just after the death of her widowed mother. Her mother died of cancer at the age of 56. Charlotte found herself thinking about her mother every night. She would often cry in her sleep. She became depressed, lost weight and became obsessed with the fear that she would never be able to adjust to her grief. She was tense and nervous at work and unable to get herself interested in anything recreational.

Charlotte was assured that she could learn how to attain the hypnotic state and relax—that if she once developed the ability to relax her body and her mind every night she would eventually be able to sleep well and would no longer have to take sleeping pills.

Many patients suffering from a distressing health-symptom will do anything for relief. She was amenable to the idea of being hypnotized and became a good hypnotic subject. She went into a state of relaxation quickly and responded favorably to suggestive therapy. Our next problem was to teach her the technique of self-hypnosis so that she could relax at home and in bed and thus sleep soundly through the night. We gave her the same instructions as described under the technique of self-relaxation. She would repeat such phrases as,

My eyes are getting very tired—very tired. Soon I will close my eyes and sleep will come.

My body is becoming more and more relaxed.

I feel all my muscles relaxing.

I am getting sleepier and sleepier and sleepier.

As I count backwards very slowly and silently starting with 100—99—98 etc. I will go into a deeper and deeper and deeper state of relaxation.

Soon the numbers will disappear and I will fall fast asleep.

When I awaken in the morning I will feel refreshed and will have had a wonderful night's sleep.

She practiced the above self-suggestions and discovered that after a week's time she was able to fall asleep without having to count.

▲ *A Case of Insomnia Caused by Feelings of Guilt.* Laura, the mother of three children, consulted her doctor because of her recent inability to sleep. As a consequence of many nights of sleeplessness she lost weight, developed a tremor of her hands and was unable to do her housework because of fatigue and general lassitude. Her doctor began to suspect her problem of insomnia was caused by emotional conflicts and recommended a psychiatric evaluation of her case.

She began using techniques of self-hypnosis and during one of her self-analytic sessions she became aware that she had been indulging in fantasies that produced feelings of guilt, which accounted for her insomnia.

"I shouldn't be thinking of such things," she said. "I feel I'm being unfaithful to my husband. I can't seem to get this certain man out of my mind. It keeps me awake."

We explained that psychic or mental infidelity need not disturb us too much. It is merely an unconscious manifestation of a basic polygamous instinct found in many of us.

She was greatly relieved when told that she need not feel

too responsible or guilty and that the less she worried, the sooner she would be able to sleep. She gave herself the following post-hypnotic suggestion.

"I can and will fall asleep." "I am going to use self-hypnosis and practice relaxing my body and my mind." "I am no longer afraid of my thoughts nor am I going to feel guilty about them." "I will keep repeating these things to myself each night until I can fall asleep without too much difficulty."

How to induce restful sleep

1. Get into the habit of going to bed at approximately the same hour each night.

2. Make sure conditions are conducive to good sleeping.

3. Practice the technique of autorelaxation 15 minutes each night.

4. Remind yourself that tension causes insomnia and that now that you are learning to relax your whole body and your mind, tension will quickly disappear as you master the art of relaxation.

5. Dismiss from your mind the thought that you cannot fall asleep. Tell yourself the opposite—that you can sleep—that you will soon fall asleep—that you are feeling sleepier and sleepier.

6. Lie still in bed and avoid as much as possible unnecessary tossing and changing of position.

7. Do not turn the lights on or get out of bed. Keep your eyes closed and keep repeating to yourself that you are getting more and more relaxed, that sleep will soon come.

8. Look forward to going to bed. Don't worry about not being able to sleep.

9. Use soft music if you find it helps to relax you.

10. Think pleasant thoughts, thoughts that are conducive to sleeping well. Relive in your sleep experiences that you enjoyed. You cannot expect to sleep soundly if you deliberately invite disturbing thoughts.

Basic points to remember

1. Insomnia is a *symptom-problem.*
2. Use autoanalysis to uncover the cause of your sleeplessness.
3. Learn to relax during the day and you will relax at night.
4. Don't bring your worries to bed with you.
5. Self-hypnosis will help you induce sleep without having to resort to sleeping drugs.
6. Practice autorelaxation every night. It helps to promote sleep.
7. Give yourself the posthypnotic suggestion that you are going to sleep soundly and awaken in the morning feeling refreshed and invigorated.

This technique has been recommended by Dora Albert, author of *Stop Feeling Tired and Start Living* (Englewood Cliffs, N. J.: Prentice-Hall, Inc., 1959). She advises her readers:

> Before you sleep, give yourself this positive mental suggestion: "I shall wake up in the morning feeling cool, calm and collected. Later in the day I shall not let anything disturb me."

Chapter Seven

What self-hypnosis can do to make your sex-life more exciting

●●

**Start with an inventory
of your sex-life**

▲ After you have induced a state of hypnotic self-relaxation concentrate on your specific sexual problem, assuming you have one. Ask yourself a series of questions. In answering them during your self-analysis stage of autohypnosis, try to develop some understanding of your particular sexual maladjustment. You will surprise yourself as to how much self-insight you can gain in this way, which will enable you to find the solution to your problem.

When a psychiatrist succeeds in getting his patient to develop insight into his own problem (referred to as "insight-therapy"), he has practically achieved half the cure. For example, if you are aware of having a faulty attitude about sex because of some neurotic parental influence, tell yourself that you can and will develop a more positive attitude. If you are living in the past, tormenting yourself with guilt feelings because of some past sexual transgression, accept the self-hypnotic suggestion that you are going to close the door to the past, forgive yourself and devote your efforts toward making a better future sexual adjustment.

What to ask yourself

1. Do I harbor guilt feelings about some past sexual experience which is interfering with my ability to enjoy sexual relations with my wife or husband?

2. Am I handicapped by a lack of adequate knowledge regarding sexual matters?

3. Is sexual disharmony the root-cause of my marital unhappiness?

4. Do I suffer from sexual immaturity?

5. Am I able to enjoy the sex act and achieve sexual satisfaction?

6. Have I been a victim of a puritanical attitude toward sex?

7. Is my lack of sexual satisfaction due to conventional shame and crippling inhibitions?

8. As a wife am I assuming my sexual responsibility as a woman by not frustrating the sexual ego of my husband?

9. As a husband do I give my wife the love and tenderness she needs to make her more responsive sexually?

10. Do I possess enough basic knowledge as to what constitutes good and bad sexual lovemaking?

11. Have I made any attempt to acquire necessary sex education knowledge?

12. What can I do to bring about an improvement in my sexual relationship with my husband or wife?

13. Am I injuring my health because of being chronically sexually frustrated?

14. Do I have a specific sexual difficulty which needs to be corrected?

15. Do I harbor any prejudices, fallacies or misconceptions about sex?

16. Do I reject my husband?

17. Do I look forward to sexual lovemaking with enthusiasm?

18. Do I occasionally take the initiative in lovemaking?

19. Am I having sexual relations too infrequently?

20. Have I invited any complications which interfere with the enjoyment of sexual relations such as infidelity, promiscuity, alcoholism?

21. Am I willing to consult a specialist for the remedy of a sexual problem particularly when all efforts at self-help have failed?

What to tell yourself

Here are 10 posthypnotic suggestions which we recommend that you repeat to yourself again—again—and again. The repetition of an idea or thought, *conditions* you to the successful acceptance and application of what you need and want to believe. You will be rewarded with sex-happiness—essential to good physical and emotional health.

1. I am convinced that attitude is all-important in understanding and correcting any sexual problem.

For Wives: I am going to enjoy the sex act; I can and will have complete sexual fulfillment whenever I have sexual relations with my husband.

For Husbands: I can and will be sexually potent with my wife and shall always be anxious for sexual relations with her.

2. I am no longer going to handicap myself with exaggerated feelings of guilt, false modesty, sexual shyness and fear of various kinds.

3. I am not going to be squeamishly self-conscious about discussing sexual matters with my husband or wife.

4. I am going to correct any misconceptions I have about various sex practices as well as eliminate any neurotic puritanical

attitudes toward sex which are handicapping my happiness in marriage.

5. I am not going to be a sexual illiterate. I can by reading a few authoritative sex manuals, improve my lovemaking technique and increase my capacity for sex-satisfaction.

6. I am going to remind myself that four-fifths of all divorces are caused by sexual incompatibility. It's not going to happen in my marriage if I can help it.

7. I am convinced that to remain sexually maladjusted and not do anything about it is to remain immature.

8. I am going to make the love relationship a reciprocal one, realizing that the mutual giving of love is the secret of sex-harmony.

9. I am going to accept the fact that frigidity and impotence are symptoms of some underlying neurosis and are curable.

10. If I suffer from some deep-seated sexual problem which I cannot resolve myself, I will be intelligent enough to seek competent professional help.

Self-hypnosis can help you develop the capacity to accept and give love

Remind yourself that you are a better lover than you think you are. Don't be obsessed with the idea that you do not have the ability to love. Learn to experience the emotion of love within yourself. You'll soon discover that you will want to and can love someone else. Self-love (the normal type) should precede man-woman love. The wife who stops loving herself also stops loving her husband.

Frigidity can be overcome with self-hypnosis

Frigidity may be defined as sexual inadequacy in women. There are many types and degrees of frigidity and many different causes.

Most authorities feel that in many instances it is caused by prudish attitudes which act as barriers to sex-satisfaction. If we accept this to be true, then we are justified in stating that frigidity is curable since wrong attitudes can be corrected.

Eric Northrup, authority on science and social psychology, in an article on sex education, reports a case that involved a woman who went to her minister, shortly after her marriage, with the tearful confession that her marriage was a failure. She said, "I am hopelessly frigid." Northrup informs us that she had gone on the night before her wedding to her aged family doctor, who had listened to her fears with parental indulgence, then disposed of the matter with the advice: "Now, don't worry. Mother Nature will take care of everything." It required several weeks before the minister could impress upon this woman that frigidity often is the result of early parental warnings that sex is "nasty" or "painful." In this particular case the woman's mother had frightened her daughter, conveying the impression that marriage involved "painful submission" for women.

There would be less frigidity if more women would heed the words of the late clergyman, Dr. Peter Marshall, who wrote: "Next to hunger, the most powerful of human instincts is that of sex. You cannot escape from it, for you are made that way. It pulses in your blood, sings in your throat, and shines in your eyes...There is nothing shameful about the sex urge."

Incidentally, it has been estimated that over 50 per cent of those who go to a minister for counsel are troubled by some problem related to sex behavior. It is gratifying that clergymen of various church denominations are fully aware of the need for premarital counseling in sexual matters and are helping to correct faulty attitudes about sex.

Some authorities claim that there are no truly frigid women. There are only those who are sexually uninformed or misinformed and men who are inexperienced and selfish. According to Dr. Albert Ellis, author of numerous books on the subject, "Literally millions of husbands are not satisfying their wives simply because they know so little of female anatomy and psychology."

Before a woman attempts self-hypnosis for a problem of frigidity we recommend that she avail herself of a complete physical examination by her physician. Let him rule out any organic cause for the frigidity. While 90 per cent of all cases of frigidity are caused by psychological factors, we also know that chronic fatigue and a general rundown condition may act as predisposing causes in the development of sexual unresponsiveness.

The sex act is both a physical and psychological experience. Tension before and during the sex act impedes one's capacity to achieve complete satisfaction.

Applying the technique of self-hypnosis, you not only enjoy the coital act yourself but you are able to make sexual lovemaking more satisfying to your partner. Once again let us repeat that relaxation becomes a habit only if you practice it. You must never become discouraged. Keep working at it. You will eventually be able to relax without any conscious effort to do so. It will become your natural way of doing everything. Self-hypnosis will also help you to concentrate during lovemaking.

Suggest to yourself during your self-therapy sessions that you are going to re-educate yourself in sexual matters and become intelligently informed. Book knowledge will assist you to analyze and better understand the cause of your particular sexual difficulty.

Here are a few books we recommend that you read:

1. *Sex and Love*
   By F. S. Caprio
   Parker Publishing Co.
   Englewood Cliffs, N. J.

2. *Helping Yourself With Psychiatry*
   By F. S. Caprio
   Prentice-Hall, Inc.
   Englewood Cliffs, N. J.

3. *The Sexually Adequate Male*
   By F. S. Caprio
   Citadel Press
   New York, N.Y.

4. *The Sexually Adequate Female*
   By F. S. Caprio
   Citadel Press
   New York, N. Y.

5. *Sex Without Guilt*
   By Albert Ellis, Ph.D.
   (Paperback edition)
   Hillman Periodicals
   New York, N. Y.

6. *Sexual Behavior (Psycho-Legal Aspects)*
   By F. S. Caprio and Donald Brenner, L.L.B.
   Citadel Press
   New York, N. Y.

In your autotherapy sessions repeat all of the posthypnotic suggestions we just recommended until you begin to experience a definite improvement in your sexual responses.

What if your husband is at fault? Self-hypnosis should enable you to develop the courage to bring the matter to his attention. You must be tactful in your approach and not belittle or humiliate him. Decide beforehand how you are going to talk to him about his method of lovemaking. If he is suffering from an impotence problem, or uses faulty technique of any kind, you are entitled to discuss the matter with him and expect his cooperation. If he deliberately refuses to cooperate despite your use of tact and diplomacy, then we recommend that you seek professional advice. Don't let any problem of sexual incompatibility go on and on without doing something constructive about it. Sex-happiness is the mortar that holds the bricks of love together.

▲ *Mabel's Problem of Frigidity.* Mabel claimed she was in love with her husband, but despite how much she loved him she was unable to achieve an orgasm during sexual relations. She consulted two gynecologists who assured her there was no physical condition to account for her frigidity. She thought at first that she was born that way, that some women just don't have any feeling or sensation in the vagina, and that it was best to try to become reconciled to this fact and not worry about it. This is what she had been told by some of her married women friends who confessed to her that they too were frigid.

Consequently, the first thing that had to be done was to make her realize that she had been *misinformed*, that frigidity is not something that is congenital. We told her also that frigidity is an illness of the subconscious and that it can be cured with self-hypnosis. She was excited to learn that she could be helped. We informed her that frigidity is a symptom-complex, the result of some one or more factors in one's past life and that these contributing influences could be recalled under hypnosis. We assured her that once she began to understand why and how her frigidity developed, she would be able to adopt a new attitude toward sex and would be able to relax and achieve sexual satisfaction for the first time. Incidentally, this latter information was given to her while she was in a state of hypnotic relaxation.

After one or two preliminary sessions of hypnosis, at a given word-signal she was able to induce her own hypnotic state of relaxation. She had practiced at home the various suggestibility tests mentioned in this book and was anxious to begin her session of autoanalysis.

Experiences from her past. She recalled an experience that occurred when she was 10 years old. She was on her way home from school when she saw a man open his trousers behind a tree and call to her. She became frightened and ran home to tell her mother. She remembers her mother reporting the incident to the police over the telephone. Afterward her mother told her that men did bad and ugly things. During her high school years a girl once kissed her on the lips. Nothing else happened but she remembered feeling kind of "funny" about it. When she learned about homosexuality in later years, she worried, thinking she had homosexual tendencies. She has had occasional dreams of a homosexual nature. At the age of 19 she was raped by a cousin. She told her mother about it. Her mother had her examined by a physician and was relieved when she was told she was not pregnant.

At home, during subsequent sessions of self-analysis in a hypnotic state she remembered that whenever she had relations with her husband she was unable to relax. She felt "unclean." She associated sex with something she had to endure rather than enjoy. She felt "held back." She loved her husband, enjoyed being kissed by him, but when he began the sex act, something happened to her. She couldn't bring herself around to participating in the love play—"I turned to stone. I felt nothing. I would tell my husband not to wait for me."

How self-hypnosis solved Mabel's problems. We put into writing for her a few suggestions she could repeat to herself during autohypnosis sessions at home. Suggestions such as:

I have gained a better understanding of my problem. I know now that I am not really frigid, that I am a warm person and that the sex act is an expression of love.

I am going to be more enthusiastic and active during love-making with my husband.

I am going to close my eyes and concentrate on the pleasurable sensations I am experiencing during the sex act.

I am not going to have any doubts about being normal sexually.

I am going to relax and allow the orgasm to occur without my getting tense or trying too hard to achieve an orgasm.

I am going to abandon myself during the sex act and experience a feeling of "total sexual surrender" reminding myself that whatever a husband and wife do to express their love for each other is normal and good.

I am not frigid and I can achieve an orgasm.

Mabel has finally succeeded in getting sexual satisfaction. She attributes her success to her complete change of attitude about sex, to the fact that she developed confidence in herself through self-hypnosis, believing that she would reach a climax. She says that the insight into the cause of her frigidity helped immensely and the self-given suggestions—that sex was something to be enjoyed—that it is an expression of love—enabled her to relax and achieve orgasms.

We hope that the many thousands of other women who are disturbed and frustrated because of this same problem will be encouraged to put self-hypnosis to the test. One thing we know —it cannot do harm. It can only do good. Self-hypnosis is bound to *improve* your sex-life. If you doubt this, try it.

▲ *Another Case Illustration of a Frigidity Problem Solved With Self-Hypnosis.* Here is Maureen's description in her own words of how she applied self-hypnosis to improve her sex-life and achieve sexual satisfaction.

> For me, the most difficult part of achieving an orgasm was the convincing of myself that it was a possibility. I could not do this, and it was not for want of desire or for effort spent. If a woman has spent five years practicing the sex act as to varieties of position, moods, etc., has read between 15 and 20 sex manuals, and still has had no results, she obviously must seek help elsewhere. Such a woman was myself.
>
> My biggest mistake was waiting until I was so buried in failure and frustration that I was positive that even if there was hope for every other frigid woman in the whole world, there was none for me. It was in this frame of mind that I went to see Dr. Caprio.
>
> He taught me to relax and to have faith and confidence in myself. He taught me that I was not different, that I was as capable of enjoying sex as any other woman. He taught me to suggest these things to myself at home.
>
> Gradually, the ideas began to penetrate and I began to

have a more positive outlook on not just sex, but on life altogether. I went to a gynecologist to be sure I was getting any necessary medical help. Gradually, I became a better sex partner and I began getting results.

For me, it was a matter of saying over and over, "Yes, I can. I know I can." This is how self-hypnosis worked for me. If you tell yourself enough times, you will believe it, and if you believe it, it will happen. And if it happened for me, it can happen for anyone.

Self-hypnosis and the single girl

Every single girl has problems of one kind or another—sex conflicts, lonesomeness, career difficulties, worries about getting married, and many others.

The number of single women who become spinsters runs into hundreds of thousands. Some girls have fewer opportunities to marry because they live in rural areas or small communities. But many fail to help themselves. They may be suffering from faulty attitudes about sex, men and marriage, or they allow their inner conflicts to interfere with making the most of an opportunity. They do nothing to make themselves more eligible for marriage. This is where self-hypnosis can help.

A single girl must implant in her subconscious mind a strong *desire* to marry. She must tell herself that she *will* marry, that love will come into her life. She has to start out with a positive attitude about sex, love and marriage. If she dislikes men, if she fears sex, if she feels that most marriages fail, her chances of finding someone to love her are slim.

Autohypnosis can give you this *positive* attitude—the confidence to seek and find love. As we have pointed out in this book, it can improve your personality and make you more appealing to the opposite sex. Self-hypnosis can help you develop enough maturity to handle any sexual problems you may have, and handle them wisely.

Too many single girls are depending on Fate to change their

status. Fate no doubt, does bring people together. But the single girl can do much to prepare herself for that lucky day when she meets her husband-to-be.

The single girl is better able to analyze herself, using techniques of self-hypnosis. With a better understanding of herself, she can correct whatever aspects of her personality are handicapping her chances for happiness.

The single girl who drinks to excess, who doesn't hold her liquor well, needs self-hypnosis. The girl who gives her date the impression that she is promiscuous or has nymphomaniac tendencies, needs self-hypnosis. The single girl who is overaggressive, oversensitive, tactless, sarcastic or complains constantly about her health isn't helping her chances of finding "the right man." She can use a bit of self-hypnosis.

If you give a house that's for sale a coat of paint, improve the landscaping and make it look its best, you are more apt to attract the right buyer. Every man wants to marry a girl who's going to be an asset to him. The reverse, of course, is also true. Bachelors could very well benefit from the same advice. Many single men can be classified as "unmarriageable" or poor marriage-risks only because they refuse to purge themselves of personality-traits that scare women away.

We would like to recommend that both sexes avail themselves of self-hypnotic techniques to improve their personalities, which should increase their eligibility for a happy marriage.

The use of self-hypnosis for the problem of impotence

Impotence is an all-encompassing term for sexual inadequacy in the male. Like frigidity there are various types of impotence. Inability to become sexually aroused, failure to carry out the sex act, lack of sex desire, premature or hasty ejaculation are only a few of the many kinds of impotence reactions.

Autoanalysis will often reveal the causative emotional factors responsible for the development of this particular sexual disorder. In questioning yourself during a session of self-analysis, keep in mind the following factors that can cause you to experience difficulty in achieving sexual fulfillment: sex-ignorance, inhibitory influences, sexual bashfulness, fear, guilt feelings, insecurity, faulty attitudes toward sex, homosexual conflicts, fear of making a woman pregnant, fear of causing a woman pain, dislike of contraceptives, fear of being seen or interrupted during the sex act and numerous other causes.

Ask yourself if your impotence is caused by some specific frustration involving your wife. If it is, discuss the matter with her and enlist her cooperation. Use auto-reconditioning to make yourself less sensitive. Letting little things bother you can diminish your sexual potency.

Understanding the specific cause of impotence makes it easier to respond successfully to self-hypnosis.

What we said about frigidity applies to the problem of impotence. One should rule out *physical* causes. Your doctor is the best qualified person to tell you if your impotence is caused by some condition that requires medical treatment. In the majority of cases, impotence is due to *psychological* causes.

Self-hypnosis can prove very effective in removing mental blocks responsible for sexual inadequacy. It can restore your confidence in your ability to perform. Your posthypnotic suggestions must be along lines of removing fears, having confidence in your technique of lovemaking, knowing that you are going to enjoy the sex act, that you are in command of your own feelings and attitudes. The repetition of these thoughts under a self-induced hypnotic state paves the way toward restoring your potency.

▲ *Harold Finally Solved His Sexual Problem With Self-Hypnosis.* Some husbands use the male menopause as an excuse for their loss of interest in sexual relations. In the following case the husband developed neurotic health ailments which he used as an alibi for his sexual apathy or indifference. When the health symptoms are subjective in origin and have no organic basis, the condition is sometimes referred to as "psychic invalidism."

Harold began calling his doctor, telling him that he suffered from indigestion, irritability and general nervousness. His doctor found nothing wrong with him physically, but he continued to complain of tension and thought that he was about to suffer a nervous breakdown, attributing it to overwork. Actually, he had little responsibility at work and plenty of time for relaxation in the evenings. Inquiring into his sex-life, we learned that Harold had a tendency to deny any connection between his sex-life and the way he felt physically. He stated:

> My sex-life is all right. Of course, I don't have sexual relations with my wife as frequently as I did, but I have no conflicts about my diminished virility.

As soon as Harold learned techniques of self-hypnosis, which he began to put into practice, he learned that he was not really suffering from the fear of a nervous breakdown, but from the fear of impotence, and that his health complaints were but a manifestation of his anxiety concerning his potency. Realizing this, he began to change for the better. He assured himself during self-hypnosis that potency is a matter of mental attitude. He resumed regular sexual relations and his symptoms began to disappear.

Summing it all up

1. Self-hypnosis can help you achieve a normal well-adjusted sex-life. It is up to you. It can help you become a better co-participant during lovemaking.

2. Through posthypnotic suggestion you can remove inhibitions which tend to impede your capacity to enjoy the sex act.

3. If you have a specific sexual problem such as impotence, frigidity or any other sexual difficulty you can employ techniques

of self-hypnosis to uncover the cause of your trouble and suggest to yourself the measures you need to take to resolve your particular sexual problem. Think of yourself via the technique of visual-imagery as an adequate responsive wife or as an adequate virile male.

4. Convince yourself that impotence and frigidity are curable conditions.

5. Believe strongly that you are capable of performing, of loving and of making your partner feel loved.

6. To become a lover, feel and act like a lover. Visualize yourself in the role of a lover.

7. Regard sex not merely as a physical act but as a mutual expression of love.

Chapter Eight

You can overcome
nervous tension, pain,
and chronic tiredness
with self-hypnosis

●●

Learn all about "tension"

▲ Remember that tension arises in people who live a fast-paced life—an unbalanced life. They lack health-intelligence and health-wisdom.

Learn what tension is, where it comes from and what you can do to overcome feelings of tenseness. Knowledge about anything gives you greater power to combat it.

Dr. George S. Stevenson, National and International Consultant for the National Association for Mental Health, and Harry Milt, the Association's Public Relations Director, have co-authored a book entitled *Master Your Tensions and Enjoy Living Again.** You'll learn a great deal about tension from these excellently qualified authors. For example, they recommend the following eight successful *Tension-Breaking Habits:*

* George S. Stevenson & Harry Milt, *Master Your Tensions and Enjoy Living Again* (Englewood Cliffs, N. J.: Prentice-Hall, Inc., 1959).

Tension-Breaker No. 1: Talk it out.
Tension-Breaker No. 2: Escape for a while.
Tension-Breaker No. 3: Take one thing at a time.
Tension-Breaker No. 4: Get rid of your anger.
Tension-Breaker No. 5: Curb the Superman urge.
Tension-Breaker No. 6: Take a positive step forward.
Tension-Breaker No. 7: Do something for someone else.
Tension-Breaker No. 8: Knock down the barbed wire fences.

How to control tension-reactions

About a year ago we encountered a most unusual experience that entailed both hypnosis and autohypnosis. A young man who had been referred to us by someone we had helped, called long distance and asked if we could give him a session of hypnosis over the telephone. He explained that he was on his way to a Western university to report for an oral examination, one of the requirements he had to meet before he could receive his Master's degree. He had completed his thesis and it had been approved and accepted. He had fulfilled all his other requirements. However, he kept postponing the date for his oral examination, in which he would have to "defend" his thesis by answering whatever questions were put to him by a group of faculty members.

He panicked at the thought of having to face these examiners. "What if I make a bad showing?"—"What if my mind goes blank?"—"What if I get nervous and am unable to give them the kind of an answer they want?" These and many other thoughts plagued him. He realized he couldn't go on putting off what he had to face someday if he wanted his M.A. degree—something he had worked very hard for.

Prior to calling us, he committed himself to a definite date and so informed the faculty. As the time for his departure approached, he became more and more tense and apprehensive. For several nights he had tossed in bed wondering what they were going to ask him. He began to have doubts as to whether he was adequately prepared for the ordeal. Nevertheless, he was determined to go through with it this time. He had read about hypnosis and was eager to be helped. It was impossible, so he claimed, to come to Washington for his session. Not having any alternative, we agreed to try it by phone.

We began by explaining that all hypnosis is really self-hypnosis, that he had to teach himself to eliminate tension and conquer what we termed "anticipatory anxiety" (the fear that not all may go well—a fear of the worst happening). We consoled him by informing him he was not alone in this problem, that many, many individuals go through this panic-like state just before making a speech or taking an examination or doing anything that is tension-producing. We further consoled him by stating that this panic or anxiety state before an examination could definitely be conquered by the individual himself—that he had it in his power to reduce tension to its minimum, which would enable him to do relaxed and clear thinking.

We then proceeded to explain over the phone in a separate session the technique of self-relaxation, how to practice increasing his receptivity to suggestion so that he would accept his own positive thoughts. We suggested that in his self-analysis sessions he try to analyze why he feared taking his orals, and why he thought he would fail them. Was he fully prepared? Had he studied enough? Did he think the professors wanted to flunk him deliberately? Was he afraid of one particular examiner? In other words we suggested that he leave no stone unturned, that he try to ferret out the root cause of his anxiety. Our last instruction was to have him write down a list of positive suggestions he was going to give himself and to repeat them en route to the university until he believed everything he needed to believe.

Upon his return he told us it wasn't half as bad as he had anticipated. He admitted beforehand to his examiners that he was a bit nervous, but that he had studied hard and hoped that he would pass. They treated him with all the sympathy and consideration they could give him. He was later notified that he had passed. His experience with autohypnosis has inspired him to apply the technique he learned to his daily life, particularly when he is confronted with any kind of fear-producing situation.

Alleviation of pain with hypnosis

Drs. William S. Kroger and S. Charles Freed in an article, "Hypnotic Control of Menstrual Pain," describe four cases of dysmenorrhea or painful menstruation treated successfully by hypnosis and posthypnotic suggestion.

In the following case history (one of the four cases) the patient was instructed as to what suggestions she should give herself (self-hypnosis) while in the hypnotic state.

> Miss L. S., aged 17, had painful menses since the age of nine and a half. The menses were always irregular. She was forced to retire to bed for 24 to 36 hours after the onset of the pain which usually occurred about 12 hours after the period began. It consisted of acute lower abdominal cramps accompanied by considerable nervousness, nausea and tension. She had received extensive therapy including dilatation and curettage, analgesics and endocrine preparations.
>
> On August 2, deep hypnosis was easily induced. Suggestions were given to the effect that her next menses would be free from discomfort; that every night before going to sleep she would say to herself, "I will have no pain. I have no dread and anticipation for my next period." These suggestions under hypnosis were repeated seven times between August 2 and August 29. The period began on September 6, and was remarkably free from pain although there were slight cramps. She did not have to go to bed. After four hypnotic treatments at weekly intervals, using the same suggestions, her next menses, on October 11, was entirely normal in every respect. For one year, without any further treatments, she has been free from pain, nervousness and all menstrual discomfort. In addition her periods have been regular.

Hypnosis and the medical world

In an article entitled "Hypnosis" published in *The American Weekly* section of *The Washington Post* (January 1, 1960), Ann Cutler, the author, reports:

> At a recent American Medical Association convention thousands of doctors from every part of the United States gathered in Atlantic City to hear the latest findings in medicine. So enthusiastic has been the acceptance of medical hypnosis by the medical profession that it is estimated that more than 10,000 doctors, psychologists, psychiatrists and dentists who have had training in the use of hypnotic techniques are using it in their daily practice. The positive results are phenomenally high.

Regarding the successful benefits of self-hypnosis, the author cites the case of Mr. M., an important Wall Street executive, whose blood pressure "shot up to 240 when the market went off or one of his special projects failed to work. He had been on medication with poor results. His family doctor, trained in the use of hypnosis in medicine decided to try it on his executive patient.

"At the first session Mr. M's blood pressure went down from 240 to 231. But the following week he was able to go deeper into hypnosis and his pressure dropped to 175. From then on he was on the mend so much so that he has been taught self-hypnosis and now puts himself under in moments of tension."

What you should know about "nervous fatigue"

Fatigue is universal. Every human being becomes tired. Normal fatigue is a protective device. It forces individuals to rest. Nature takes care of this normal tiredness through the mechanism of sleep. But there is a type of chronic or exaggerated tiredness which psychiatrists refer to as a mental or nervous fatigue, a body-mind reaction or state caused by tension-like hate or anger. Nervous fatigue handicaps us from enjoying life, from accomplishing the things we want to do. It causes us to be unhappy and irritable. When we are unhappy we are tired.

Self-therapeutic suggestions for the release of tension-fatigue

1. *I am going to autocondition my mind every morning with a positive attitude toward each new day.*

Don't start the day with trepidation. We have had patients who claim they would gag and become nauseated every morning just thinking about having to go to work. Their attitude was a negative one. It was no wonder they experienced tension-headaches. They disliked their jobs, complained about their aches and pains and experienced boredom because of the monotony of day-to-day living. Every day was a battle to be won. This kind of attitude in the struggle to survive is bound to bring on exaggerated tiredness. We all know people who are always tired. They can sleep 10 and 12 hours and awaken tired. The truth of the matter is that they are victims of emotionally induced fatigue. They are basically unhappy—tired of living.

It is wiser to suggest to yourself every morning, "I am glad to be alive. Every day is another interesting adventure. Life is a challenge." Instead of complaining tell yourself, "I am going to do my best with each situational-problem as it arises."

2. *I am going to learn to do everything in a relaxed way.*

It is not the amount of work you do but the manner in which you do that work that's tiring. Don't try to crowd into a day's agenda more than you can accomplish well. Budget your energy. Don't work in excess of a reasonable number of hours. An excess of anything is unwise. For example, an excess of coffee, cigarettes or alcohol only increases nervous tension.

3. *I am going to develop an outside interest.*

Working at something you do not particularly like or are not fitted for makes you tired. If you must continue at this work because of its compensations or because no other job is available, then plan for the development of some outside recreational interest. If yours is a sitting job, seek your recreation in tennis, golf, swimming or dancing. If your job requires constant use of your arms or legs, seek rest through bridge, the theatre, automobile riding or reading a book. The monotony of mechanical living, doing the same thing day in and day out—coming home, eating and feeling tired and going to bed early—is bound to have a demoralizing effect. A change from the day's monotony is what you need for happy, healthy living. Some diversion every week is desirable. Often planning for that trip, that party or that sport brings as much pleasure and relaxation as the event itself. It is the breaking away from the grind, exercising dormant muscles and refreshing one's thoughts that brings healing rest.

4. *I am going to keep my negative emotions under control.*

Anger, hatred, jealousy, sorrow, anxiety, envy and crying spells are expressions of *emotionalism*. They are abnormal reactions giving rise to "emotional intoxication." They dissipate your mental strength and in turn cause *tension-fatigue*.

Don't become high-geared, sensitive, nervous, irritable, subject to emotional outbursts. Learn to be tolerant, cooperative and above all cheerful. A spell of the "blues" can tire one more quickly than actual work.

Unhappiness saps vitality. Suggest to yourself repeatedly that controlling your emotions means conserving your energy (emotional economy).

5. *I am going to cultivate healthy living habits.*

Irregular living, improper food, loss of sleep, lack of exercise, all help to bring about a state of chronic tiredness. If you suffer from insomnia, find the cause and eliminate it. Insomnia favors the development of tension-fatigue. The average individual requires eight hours of sleep. Avoid overeating. It makes you mentally sluggish.

What the ability to relax will mean:

1. You will experience better physical health.
2. You will be able to get along better with people.
3. You will be able to do clearer thinking.
4. You will be less fatigued at the end of the day.
5. You will have a happier marital relationship.
6. You will become more tolerant.
7. You will live longer.

The worry habit
and what you can do about it

Here are some facts about the worry habit and how you can use self-hypnosis to dispel "worrisome thoughts":

1. Excessive worrying about anything is an *acquired habit.* Worry isn't a trait that's inherited. If we are around people who worry too much we are inclined to develop the same habit. Parents who are fearful generally project their anxieties and fears onto their children. When the children grow up they find themselves *imitating* their parents. Worry is *contagious.* You don't have to *imitate* a neurotic's way of thinking.

2. Excessive worrying doesn't solve your problem. Making yourself sick over something only makes the matter worse.

3. Chronic worrying is a symptom of insecurity—evidence of a lack of self-confidence.

4. The worry-habit is like any other habit—that can be conquered if once you make up your mind.

5. Remind yourself that worry is a dissipation of nervous energy. It is fatigue-producing—health-destroying.

6. Try to analyze and understand the problem you are worrying about and what caused it, using the technique of hypnotic self-analysis.

7. Devote your energy to working out ways of solving your

problem. Doing something about something is more intelligent than worrying and doing nothing about it.

8. Some people aren't happy unless they have something to worry about. Psychiatrists refer to them as *masochists*. They seem to enjoy negative thinking—only because they are in ignorance of the far greater joy that comes with mental control. Tell yourself that you are not going to become one of these masochistic worriers.

9. Profit by what George Hawkes, a former Dean of Columbia College, Columbia University, wrote. He counseled almost a fifth of a million students who came to him with their troubles:

> Half the worry in the world is caused by people who try to make a decision before they have sufficient knowledge on which to base a decision. If a man will devote his time to securing all the facts related to his problem his worries will usually evaporate in the light of knowledge.

Develop a sense of humor— it's a tension-reducer

Tell yourself: "I am going to convince myself that a sense of humor is an antidote to worry. It will help me achieve an even disposition and is as essential to intelligent living as food is for survival."

A healthy portion of laughter can make the daily grind less tedious. It is a mechanism for easing strain. It converts saggy muscles and saddened eyes into a refreshing smile. Give yourself these three suggestions:

1. "I need to laugh for the maintenance of good health, for the relaxation of my mind and body. I am going to remind myself not to take either myself or my troubles too seriously. Laughter will help make life more bearable. Laughter is a habit. I am capable of cultivating it by simply repeating each day that I will find something to laugh about.

" 'The great purpose of life,' remarked Oliver Wendell Holmes, 'is to live it.' Whether my fears are real or imaginary I will find them less awesome if I strive to participate in the great happenings in the world around me. I am not going to nurse my own fears and unhappiness. If I would have happiness, I must embrace my world, know and learn what makes it 'tick.' I am going to interest myself in my friends and my family —share their joys and I will be joyful too."

2. "I am going to make a positive effort to enjoy life, based on the principle that happiness is an *attitude* that can be *cultivated*. It will teach me to expect sorrows and misfortunes, but at the same time give me the courage to survive them."

3. "I am no longer going to live in constant tension, afraid to relax, seldom allowing myself to smile and spending much of my time living in the unhappy past. I am going to make day-to-day living pleasurable."

Salient points

1. Nervous tension associated with nervous fatigue is a handicap in life, affecting not only physical health, but mental happiness.

2. Unhappiness is one of the greatest causes of nervous tension.

3. To prevent nervous tension try to keep your mind relaxed and free of any unpleasantness that tends to keep you upset. Feed your mind pleasant thoughts.

4. Use self-hypnotic techniques to relax your muscles. Body-relaxation produces mind-relaxation.

5. Remind yourself to laugh a little every day.

6. Everyone needs recreational relaxation. Relaxation benefits everyone.

7. Enrich your life with spare-time hobbies.

8. Make life easier for yourself.

9. Keep in mind that life is to be enjoyed.

Chapter Nine

Master your emotions
through self-hypnosis

●●

How to control fear
through self-hypnosis

▲ The best way to conquer any fear is to study and understand it. As we have said many times, "Knowledge is power." To know why you are afraid and how your fear developed is half the battle. If you wish to overcome a particular morbid fear or phobia use the four-step method of self-hypnosis. Ask yourself during autoanalysis:

Is my fear a conditioned reaction to some early unpleasant reaction?

For example, a patient related how at the age of 12, she discovered a mouse under her pillow. She was frightened and screamed. Her brother had placed it there as a prank. Ever since this particular episode she has had nightmares and awakens terrified at the thought of a mouse under her pillow.

Ask yourself also: *"Is my fear a substitute or disguised fear of something else?"*

An unmarried girl who had a morbid fear of dirt (misophobia) found it necessary to wash her hands over and over again.

In studying her case it was discovered that her true or sub-conscious fear was fear of moral contamination.

Oftentimes the abnormal fear represents a symbol of something that is unpleasant and repressed. The phobia serves a definite function. It is intended to disguise or displace an entirely different fear, one which is too painful to our consciousness. In other words, a morbid fear is a form of escape mechanism from some inner mental conflict. Morbid fears can often be traced to early repressed or forgotten experiences.

Self-analysis can help you trace the origin of your abnormal fear or phobia. While in the self-induced hypnotic state you should be able to recall the causative traumatic episode that you had forgotten or repressed which may have been responsible for your present fear.

This process of re-living emotionally the original fear, un-covering the subconscious meaning of the fear, using techniques of self-hypnosis, should relieve you of anxiety symptoms. You can follow this with such posthypnotic suggestions as "Fear is common to all human beings." "I am no longer afraid to be afraid." "Morbid fears can be controlled by understanding them, acknowledging them and doing something about them. I am going to treat my fears as *bad habits*. I am going to reassure myself that self-hypnosis can help me break the fear habit, just as it can help me break any other unwanted habit."

**How to use self-hypnosis
to conquer a bad temper**

Tell yourself during your sessions of self-hypnosis:

1. Anger is an abnormal emotion.

2. Only a person who is emotionally immature gives way to outbursts of anger.

3. Expressing anger accomplishes nothing. It is a dissipation of energy.

4. I believe that my bad temper *can* be controlled, and I am not going to rationalize by thinking that I cannot help myself.

5. Getting angry easily is a trait that has become a habit.

6. Whenever I find myself getting baited into a heated argument I will change the subject or will remind myself to remain calm and realize the other person may have reasons for feeling as he does.

7. I am not going to be fooled into thinking that repressing anger is harmful. Control is something different from repression; it involves self-confidence, understanding and wisdom.

8. When I feel myself getting angry I am quickly going to give myself the suggestion that I can switch my thoughts to something else.

9. If need be, I can always walk away from the person who is provoking the anger reaction, or expend my energy in doing something that will divert my mind—finding some other outlet for my pent-up emotions.

10. I will count to 10 slowly and then give myself the suggestion that I have my emotions under control.

11. If the other person gets angry I will remind myself that this is all the more reason I should keep calm. (Incidentally, this was Benjamin Franklin's advice to people who are susceptible to anger.)

12. Whenever possible I will try to laugh off a situation that is getting too serious by resorting to a sense of humor. I will remind myself that it never pays to take myself or my problems too seriously.

13. I am going to practice the technique of autorelaxation whenever I find myself in a situation that may precipitate an argument.

14. I am going to autosuggest the idea that I have a permanent immunity to people who deliberately try to upset me.

15. I am going to remind myself that people can make me

angry only if I let them, and that to become angry is to flatter
the other person.

16. I am going to think with my mind and not with my
emotions.

You can relax away sick emotions

Anger, hate, selfishness, fear, suspicion, vanity, jealousy, are
emotions that can make *you* sick. As we mentioned in the previous chapter, they cause "emotional intoxication," which dis-
sipates your mental energy.

In an article entitled "Cancer and Your Emotions" (*Cosmopolitan* magazine, April 1960), the author, T. F. James, reports
that grief, depression, hostility, anger and aggressiveness seem
to influence one's susceptibility to cancer. He found that many
cancer patients have a certain type of personality-profile and that
emotional stress plays a significant role in the development of
the disease.

This fact alone should be reason enough for you to learn to
master your emotions. You can accomplish this by daily practicing the technique of autorelaxation.

Give yourself a session at the beginning of each day, suggesting that you are going to remind yourself to exercise self-control
throughout the day, that you are going to practice tolerance
and think and do everything "the relaxed way."

▲ *How Hypnosis Led Joyce to "The Open Road."* Joyce,
who had once been a victim of negative emotions, brought in
the following account of her return to "The Open Road."

> In attempting to assemble my thoughts toward expressing
> what self-hypnosis has done for me, strangely enough, I
> find myself returning to a poem of Walt Whitman's
> which I, in younger days and in difficult times, turned to
> time and again, repeating it to myself, to give me a re-
> newed strength of purpose. The poem is called,

THE OPEN ROAD

> Afoot and lighthearted I take to the open road,
> Healthy, free, and the world before me,
> The long brown path before me
> Treading wherever I choose.
> Henceforth I ask not good fortune
> I myself am good fortune
> Strong and content I travel the open road.

I feel that self-hypnosis has led me again to the open road. I know that the fears, sorrows, apprehensions, and misdirected thoughts were the exemplary weeded growth of a challenge of which I was not being the master. I learned to look objectively upon my everyday experiences as small and useful building blocks of character.

Upon realization of this fact, I was able to feel the freedom which prevaded it in all its length and breadth, and the challenge which beckoned at its horizon. Self-hypnosis has enabled me to continue my journey and by-pass the by-roads.

Self-hypnosis and morbid fears

Every psychiatrist encounters cases of "cardiophobia"—people who worry about their heart. They become obsessed with the idea that they have a heart disorder of some kind. They suffer from a state of chronic anxiety, which in turn begins to affect the normal heart.

The following excerpt appeared in the *Chicago Daily News*, February 8, 1956:

> There are more people who think they have heart disease —and don't—than who actually have it, a heart specialist said...
>
> Dr. Edward Weiss of Philadelphia said these are frequently the most difficult patients to treat.
>
> They are beset with anxieties and tensions in their per-

sonal lives. The heart becomes the focal point because it
is the traditional seat of emotions.

One of the doctor's toughest jobs is to separate the
patients who have physical heart disease from those who
only fear they do, because they, too, develop many of the
symptoms—shortness of breath, fatigue, pain in the chest.

It isn't enough for the doctor to tell the patient that
there's nothing wrong with his heart, Dr. Weiss said to a
conference for general practitioners sponsored by the Chicago Heart Association...

He must try to determine why the patient has the symptoms and help him with his problems.

Otherwise the patient's emotional factors will go on to
make his life and his family miserable, Dr. Weiss said.

Autohypnosis can help many such individuals who have a
phobia of heart disease, a phobia of cancer, polio, brain tumor,
or some other disease. The elimination of tension via the method
of hypnotic self-relaxation usually cures the patient of his phobia,
since tension and abnormal fears are closely interrelated.

▲ A *Self-Cured Case of Claustrophobia.* Mrs. Baxter, a
woman in her late thirties, described how she was able to conquer her fear of closed spaces (claustrophobia) by means of
self-hypnosis.

> I was afraid to get into elevators. Whenever I was caught
> in a crowd I felt I would suffocate. I couldn't remain in a
> room without having to open the door or a window. The
> thought of being hemmed in threw me into a panic.
>
> After I learned the technique of placing myself in a
> hypnotic state I was able to trace my phobia to its root
> cause. When I was 12 years of age, two of my playmates
> induced me to get into a wooden box. They sat on the lid
> of the box and wouldn't let me out until I had screamed
> for help. I thought I was going to die. My mother finally
> rescued me.
>
> I have given myself the repeated suggestion that I can

now ride in elevators and found that I was able to do this
without feeling panicky. Knowing that I had discovered
the cause of my phobia gave me confidence. I realized that
my fear of suffocating was nothing more than a carry-over
from this early unpleasant experience.

I am convinced that tension causes people to be afraid
of many things. I practiced the art of autohypnosis by telling myself that I could relax at will, simply by thinking
about letting my muscles go limp, and concentrating on
the thought that nothing would happen to me. I was satisfied that I had discovered the cause of my claustrophobia.

At first I would repeat to myself over and over again,
"I don't have to fear closed spaces . . . My mind can control my fear of elevators." Now I find that I no longer
have to give myself these suggestions. I no longer experience tension and consequently am no longer uneasy or
nervous in an elevator.

▲ *A Scientist Overcomes Stage Fright With Self-Hypnosis.*
Dr. E., a research scientist in his seventies, had gained an envi-
able reputation in his field. Because of his outstanding qualifications, he was invited many times to address various audiences,
but was inclined to refuse such invitations because he feared he
would become too uneasy and nervous. Once, at a convention
a year ago, he lectured to a group of scientists and experienced
palpitations of the heart, perspiration and the feeling that he
was going to faint.

He realized that fear is an emotion that is influenced by the
mind. He knew that if he could learn to control his mind, he
would in turn control his fear. He practiced autorelaxation and
kept repeating these positive autosuggestions:

> I have nothing to fear—I am going to concentrate on the
> message I wish to pass on to my audience and not on my-
> self—I have confidence in the power of my own mind.

He learned to give himself a session of self-hypnosis before every subsequent lecture and reported that he was able to give many talks afterwards with very little discomfort.

▲ *A Concert Pianist Who Used Self-Hypnosis to Control His Hand Tremor.* A young unmarried man, age 34, who had devoted most of his life to the study of music and had given several concert recitals, consulted us about a tremor of his right hand, which he had developed within the past year.

Here is his story of what he was able to accomplish with self-hypnosis:

> I was an accomplished pianist and had earned the applause of numerous audiences. During one of my recitals my mind wandered momentarily off to a certain girl I was planning to marry. We had disagreed about our marriage plans. She told me she wasn't quite sure she would go through with the marriage. In the middle of one of my recitals I experienced a feeling of panic and my right hand began to tremble. Fortunately I managed to complete my concert although I was aware that I had not done my best. I became apprehensive about giving another recital, believing that my hand tremor would reappear.
>
> I memorized the 4-A's method of self-hypnosis.
>
> During self-analysis, I began to solve the conflicts I was experiencing involving my fiancée. For one thing I was suffering from a fear of being rejected. I had always felt unsure of myself when it came to any relationship with the opposite sex. I came to the conclusion that I was too self-centered. I practiced being more considerate, humble and less anxious. I developed greater confidence in myself and my girl finally decided to go through with the marriage. Self-analysis revealed that my tremor had been caused by this frustration.
>
> My final step was to give myself the repeated posthypnotic suggestion that I would be completely relaxed and in full control of my emotions when playing the piano. I have noticed that I am playing better than ever and am happy to say that my hand tremor completely disappeared.

How to overcome the fear
of air travel with self-hypnosis

There are many persons who admit quite frankly that they are afraid to fly. They prefer some other mode of traveling. Some have never been in an airplane and attribute their prejudice against air travel to newspaper accounts of airplane crashes. They are too scared to take their first trip, and are obsessed with the idea that their first experience will be their last. If someone tries to assure them that the odds are in their favor, that considering the many thousands of air miles, which pilots cover without a mishap, they will invariably remind you of some past tragedy that made the headlines. They exclaim: "But, how can you be sure? Every time you step into a plane you are taking a chance. What about unexpected lightning storms? What about mechanical failure? There's no guarantee that you will arrive safely. In an automobile accident or even a train wreck you stand some chance of surviving. But when a plane crashes, there are seldom any survivors."

We could go on and on with this kind of negative thinking which people in this group resort to. Some of them have no desire or any intention ever to fly. They feel it is no great handicap if they never get off the ground. But there are those who do have a desire to travel by air. They wish they could overcome their fear of flying. They are aware of the many advantages of going someplace by plane. They accept their fear as a decided handicap. They don't know how to go about preparing themselves mentally for their initial flight. They imagine they would panic. The idea of being "shut in"—"having no place to run to"—"not being able to get off if they did panic," etc., blocks them from ever going to an airport.

We feel that a fear of flying, particularly in our modern times, *is* a handicap. However, we do not mean to imply that air travel is the best or only way one should travel. Every mode of travel has its special advantages. We are merely concerned with helping those who are afraid to fly and who would like to travel to Europe by air, or cross the country in an airplane or even take shorter trips, because of the time-saving factor.

The authors have had the opportunity of helping persons who came to us with this very specific problem. We discovered that self-hypnosis proved a most effective method of overcoming their fear of flying.

▲ *The Frightened Stewardess.* In one instance, an airline stewardess, who had survived a crash, stated that she had developed a fear of flying and would never fly again. She claimed that her one frightening experience left its mark. She became aware for the first time how "lucky she was," to use her own words. She felt relieved when she gave up her job and was married. Her husband, a businessman, was accustomed to traveling by air and invited her to accompany him on many of his business trips. She refused, admitting that she just couldn't make herself get in a plane again. Since her desire to share his trips was so strong, she decided to try hypnosis and proved to be a good subject.

We subjected her to the technique of abreaction, having her relive and describe under hypnosis the details of her traumatic experience. Following this she was given the posthypnotic suggestion that she would no longer live in the past, that she would be able to fly again, relaxed and comfortable and that she would overcome her fear of flying by learning how to apply and practice the 4-A's method of autohypnosis as described in this book.

She has since taken four trips by air, one to the Seattle World's Fair, another from Washington to Chicago, a trip to New Orleans (two of her husband's business trips), and a flight to Rome. She reported that she was free of any apprehension and was able to relax and enjoy each experience as she formerly had when she was a stewardess.

▲ *The Two Worried Wives.* We had two couples consult us who had made plans to fly to Spain for a brief vacation. The husbands had no problem. They had flown many times before. Both their wives were worried, feared the trip and were acutely apprehensive. Each of them had the experience of going to Florida by plane, but had never crossed the Atlantic. One of them wondered if she should take a strong sedative, thinking it would alleviate her tension. The other was superstitious and feared something would happen because the date of their departure fell on the thirteenth of the month. We instructed them as to how they could make good use of self-hypnotic suggestions and assured them that they would find every minute of their experience enjoyable.

The reader might feel disappointed if we were merely to say that the way to overcome the fear of flying is to practice the technique of hypnotic self-relaxation every day for a week before your prospective trip and all during the time you are in an airplane. Consequently, we are going to give you a few specific things to think about and suggest to yourself; these ideas should be combined with or supplement your autorelaxation, and should make it easier for you to achieve the ultimate result you desire:

1. In your day-to-day sessions of autohypnosis suggest to yourself these thoughts: that you *like* airplanes, that you are fascinated by them, that it's a wonderful way to travel, that you are fortunate to be living in an age whereby this mode of travel is available to you, that you are sharing with many thousands of other people the benefits of modern progress. Repeat them to yourself as often as you need to. This develops in you a *positive* attitude about flying. If you *dislike* something, and you keep reminding yourself how much you dislike it, it becomes far more difficult to accept or adjust to that which you dislike.

To cite an example, if a person claimed he disliked people, expressed this feeling to others, and kept repeating how much he is bored by people, naturally he is going to feel miserable and have a miserable time at every social gathering he attends. What is he accomplishing by assuming this kind of negative attitude toward people? In fact, he does himself a great deal of harm. As time goes on he takes a *negative* attitude about many other things. We all know people who are predominantly pessimistic, skeptic and negativistic. They lose friends quickly because no one wants to be exposed to someone who is "against everything," who predicts the worst and has a gloomy outlook on life.

To overcome your fear of flying, you must develop the attitude that you don't dislike traveling by air, that it will be an *adventure* for you, a new experience.

2. Condition yourself to the atmosphere of an airport. Watch the planes come and go. Observe the many people buying their tickets, having their luggage weighed, watching people being met by their friends. Capture the feeling of others. Imagine (via the technique of "visual imagery") that you are arriving by plane. Identify yourself with those you see coming and going. Picture yourself inside a plane. Tell yourself it must be wonderful to be able to travel, that it's exciting. This kind of positive autoconditioning should prepare you psychologically for your first trip.

3. Take your first trip in a plane with some other person, someone you admire and respect or, better still, with a group of friends who are planning a trip somewhere. This helps you achieve more peace of mind. You begin to console yourself that you are not alone. You begin to think, "If your friends can travel this way and not feel tense, so can I."

4. Watch the other passengers, including the stewardess. Her smile is an attempt to relax you. Remember relaxation is *contagious*. Let the relaxation of the other passengers rub off on you. Make believe you are relaxed. Smile and converse with whoever is sitting next to you. This will have a tendency to get your mind off yourself.

5. Resort to distraction gimmicks. Don't just sit there and

worry about the sound of the motors. Read an interesting book, or several articles in a magazine. Work a crossword puzzle if you like. Many businessmen become absorbed in some project or problem that requires a solution. Some women bring their knitting bag along. Or you can pass the time away chatting. Whatever it is, keep yourself mentally occupied. It's surprising how quickly time passes, especially if you are having one or two of your meals on the plane. Don't give yourself time to think about anything unfavorable happening.

6. Take advantage of the wonderful opportunity you have to practice putting yourself in a state of hypnotic relaxation. Go through the various steps in the early part of the book. Start with muscle-relaxation, followed by complete body-relaxation, with or without closing your eyes and then proceed to give yourself some of the above suggestions. Talk to yourself, silently, of course. Make up your own positive-thinking suggestions.

Here is a sample:

1. I am proud of the fact that I made myself do something I previously feared.

2. I don't have to be nervous and tense. I am capable of relaxing. I have learned how to relax my body and my mind.

3. I feel fortunate that I am able to get where I am going in such a short period of time.

4. Overcoming my fear of flying will help me overcome other fears. It will enable me to develop greater self-confidence. It will give me a sense of self-mastery.

5. I prefer not to be a chronic worrier. I am going to manifest faith in everything I do—faith in the thought that nothing will happen. My faith in a Higher Power will always come to my rescue and provide me with peace of mind.

6. I am going to make good use of my new habit of hypnotic self-induced relaxation.

7. I am going to practice relaxing each part of my body (progressive relaxation) until I have learned to master the technique

of relaxing my entire body (complete relaxation). When my body is relaxed my mind will relax. Relaxation is the best antidote for worry.

8. Instead of worrying about being afraid, I am going to do something about it. I am going to read various books explaining the psychology of fear. I am going to learn the difference between normal and abnormal fears. If I understand the facts about various fears I will be more successful in overcoming them.

These are merely sample suggestions, to give you some idea of how to go about using hypnotic autosuggestion to advantage. As we said before, you can make up your own list and make it as long as you wish, regarding what to think about or tell yourself that will put you in the proper mood for going someplace by air. If you follow everything we said above precisely, we can almost guarantee you will conquer your fear of flying. It will also be a step toward the conquest of other "unreasonable" fears.

Techniques to overcome
fear of flying

In a personal communication with Melvin Powers, he informed us that he has used the following technique in helping his subjects overcome the fear of flying.

He takes the individual to the airport and makes a tape recording of the various sounds of the airport terminal as well as other sounds of the plane itself. These sounds are played back to the individual when he is in a state of hypnosis. Posthypnotic suggestions are then given that he will feel fine, relaxed and enjoy flying in a plane.

Key things to remember

1. Fear is a protective emotional reaction to danger. Everybody experiences fear. It is normal to be afraid when there is justification to be afraid.

2. However, there are *abnormal* fears that are out of proportion to a particular threat or situation. They are called morbid fears or phobias.

3. Many phobias are disguised or substitute fears of other hidden or repressed fears.

4. Finding the cause of and understanding the symbolic meaning of a particular morbid fear through techniques of self-hypnosis is a step toward the cure.

5. Pretend not to be afraid and you will feel less afraid.

6. Self-hypnosis can help you control sick emotions (anger, hate, jealousy, revenge) as a result of which you will be rewarded with better physical and mental health.

Chapter Ten

You can defeat
mental depression
and unhappy moods
with self-hypnosis

●━●

Analyze the nature and
cause of your unhappy moods

▲ Use the following questionaire in conjunction with the third step of self-hypnosis (autoanalysis). When you are properly relaxed, begin to analyze yourself in relation to your susceptibility to becoming easily depressed.

You can find out *why* you become so moody by studying the answers to these questions:

	Yes	No
1. Am I too sensitive to criticism?	___	___
2. Are my feelings easily hurt whenever I experience the slightest rejection?	___	___
3. Do I dislike my physical appearance because of being fat, too thin, unattractive, flat-chested, or the way I talk?	___	___

	Yes	No
4. Do I get into an irritable mood when I'm very tired?	____	____
5. Am I too shy around people?	____	____
6. Do I suffer from indecision?	____	____
7. Do I lack self-confidence?	____	____
8. Do I worry about everything?	____	____
9. Am I living too much in the past?	____	____
10. Do I feel sorry for myself, seeking sympathy from my family and friends?	____	____
11. Am I quickly discouraged?	____	____
12. Am I too suspicious of people's motives?	____	____
13. Do I blame my inadequacies and difficulties on other people?	____	____
14. Am I too immature to accept ordinary responsibilities?	____	____
15. Do I classify as a health-neurotic, indulging in excessive health-complaining?	____	____
16. Do I attribute my depressed moods to some physical condition?	____	____
17. Am I unhappy and depressed because of undue resentment, disillusionment or having been hurt by someone I once loved?	____	____
18. Am I pessimistic about the future?	____	____
19. Am I obsessed with the thought that I am a victim of "hard luck"?	____	____

After you have answered the above questions write down your conclusions and decide that you are going to do something about these frequent mood swings.

What you should know
about mental depression

There are two types of depression: (1) normal and (2) morbid. All of us are susceptible to becoming depressed for one reason or another only because we are subjected to both positive and negative influences. If something good happens to us or we succeed in achieving a particular goal, we are naturally happy. On the other hand, if we become greatly disappointed or become chronically ill, we are apt to experience mental depression.

It is important to remind yourself that under certain circumstances *it is normal to become temporarily depressed.* Even psychiatrists who treat depressed patients, at times become depressed themselves. All human beings, the poor, the rich, the young, the old are subject occasionally to unhappy moods.

Many mistaken individuals believe that a normal person is someone who is blessed with good physical health, never gets mentally upset and maintains a cheerful disposition at all times. So-called "normal" people experience periods of depressions especially when they meet with a disappointment, but they manage to overcome their unhappy mood. Neurotics allow themselves to become chronically depressed, indulge in self-pity and in some instances have to be hospitalized because of the possibility of suicide.

As we just explained, disappointments in life can cause anyone to become depressed. The important thing is how to manage worries and frustrations of everyday life. We either survive them or succumb to them. If we are hypersensitive to disappointments and frustrations, we seek an outlet through the mechanism of depression—an SOS telegram for sympathy. Receiving no answer from our world of friends, we fall back on our next best alternative—self-pity.

Many of us experience states of depression because of some physical handicap or illness. The person, for example, who suffers from an ulcer may be very moody and have a sour disposition. It is understandable that someone who is told that he has an incurable disease is likely to be very depressed. One could hardly expect him to feel otherwise. However, psychiatrists know that these unfortunate victims can make their illness more endurable by adopting a peace-of-mind attitude—one of philosophical acceptance.

Many women with menstrual difficulties experience premenstrual tension and headaches and become depressed during their menstrual cycle. They very often project their unhappy moods onto their husbands and children.

The menopause often causes women to experience a change in personality. It is not too uncommon for women who are going through the menopause cycle to complain of feelings of despondency and depression with a tendency to melancholia. These same symptoms sometimes occur among middle-aged men who are going through the "Climacterium Virile" or Male Menopause. Men who develop premature sexual impotence during this period are prone to suffer from middle-age depression. The impotence is generally psychic in origin and not due to any physical or organic condition.

Premature aging causes many men to become depressed. A British doctor once said: "When a man is so ill as to think he is ill when he is not ill at all, then he is very ill indeed." This may well be paraphrased to the subject of age: When a man is so old as to think he is old when he is not old at all, then he is very old indeed.

Any physical condition is capable of influencing the mind and disposition of the individual. Likewise the mind is also capable of influencing the particular physical ailment. If a patient suffering from tuberculosis allows himself to become more and more depressed to the point of becoming pessimistic about his recovery, his chances of being cured are greatly reduced. If instead he were to assume a more hopeful mental attitude the probability of his recovery sooner would be greatly enhanced.

Whether the cause of your depression is a physical illness or an emotional frustration remember that it is unintelligent to allow yourself to remain depressed and unhappy.

Use posthypnotic suggestion to divert your mind from yourself

Dr. Henry C. Link tells a story which has been repeated many times in the experiences of every psychologist and psychiatrist. A middle-aged woman in business suffered terrific fits of depression. As these spells became more frequent her work suffered badly. An investigation confirmed the suspicion that this woman had a very limited circle of acquaintances and virtually no friends; though she worked with certain employees for years, she knew almost nothing about them. She was advised to study the people about her, to learn something of their work and families. This she did, and at last report, she was so engrossed in helping two families that she had no time for melancholy reflections.

Concentrate on ways to divert your mind away from yourself. As expressed by Dr. Charles H. Mayo:

> The mind must be treated with the same rules of care and exercise as the body. New interests, continued education and variety will keep the brain up to the pace set by the fine and durable bodies which science now endows even the aged.

Tell yourself in your self-therapy sessions:

> I am going to forget the misfortunes of the past. I am to begin to live today and enjoy the elixirs of life that are available to me. If I need a vacation I am going to take one. To spice and flavor my life as I would season my food is the magic key to the feeling of well-being.

▲ *How Mrs. Lane Conquered Her Depressed Moods With Self-Hypnosis.* Mrs. Lane, an attractive woman in her middle thirties, had made a habit of negative thinking. She was a confirmed pessimist. Despite the fact that she realized that her *depressed moods* were caused by her dark outlook on life, she experienced a sense of helplessness. She didn't know where to begin or how to bring about a change in her mental attitudes. Her eagerness to learn the techniques of self-hypnosis made her a successful hypnotic subject. She became an entirely "new person" by changing her philosophy of life. Here is her own account of how she thinks *today:*

> I will attempt to describe in the simplest way possible why I choose to make a *positive way of thinking* and *living* a part of my life. Each and every day of my life I plan to live to the fullest by thinking how fortunate I am to be alive. To begin with, I cherish every day I live and can enjoy this wonderful world of ours. I have come to the conclusion that I must think this first and primarily before I can go through each day with pleasant and optimistic thoughts. I don't permit myself to dwell on how difficult or uninteresting a particular job or chore might be. I tackle it and amaze myself that it wasn't nearly as bad as I thought it would be. Time and again I've experienced the feeling that an assignment I simply hated to begin was surprisingly simple once I actually made up my mind to get started and do something about it.
>
> When I feel particularly depressed, I think of the large number of people in this world who are physically handicapped; some have been afflicted since birth or through some unfortunate accident and must now live their lives minus a limb, eyesight, etc. I count my blessings right then and there, I say to myself, "What can I complain about and why am I complaining? I am fortunate beyond words. I have health. With this I have a treasure beyond any material thing I could possibly own." I have my health, and with this idea sincerely and genuinely es-

tablished in my thoughts, I cannot help but begin to feel grateful and happy. I have instilled in my mind through repeated autosuggestion and self-hypnosis that I have the ability to do anything within reason that I have made up my mind to do. As a result I feel not only enlightened but encouraged because I feel that in just having the gift of good health I have everything. I have come to believe that there are so many lovely amusing incidents that make up our lives. When there is a genuine and sincere interest in everything about you, there is no boredom.

At one time I would awaken in the morning with the thought: "What a dreary day I am going to have again —I'm sure everything will go wrong today." Now I realize, "How can anything be pleasant and exciting if I consider it drab and ugly before I have given myself a chance to find out what it will be like—whether I will find it enjoyable or will it suit my taste?" I stifle pessimistic thoughts and instead every morning I start getting myself in the "proper mood" for the day ahead of me. Before getting out of bed, I close my eyes, relax and concentrate on the idea that this is going to be another interesting day. If things go wrong I tell myself, "It could have been worse." As long as I think in this fashion nothing will beat me down. When I have sincerely tried and performed to the best of my ability I experience an inner contentment.

I have personally found that in applying a *positive* approach and a keen eager interest and determination to reach the goal I set out for without burdening myself with countless pros and cons about whether I can do it, I seldom fail. I try to be myself, enjoy what the other person has to tell me, listen intently and I cannot help but enjoy whatever I happen to be doing at the moment. In other words, if I am eating an apple, I eat it leisurely and savor the taste. I don't rush to gulp it down, as I had been doing. I take my time and enjoy it to the fullest. I repeat over and over again the suggestion that my life is controlled and regimented by myself, as to whether I make it lovely and happy is controlled by me and me alone.

Take, for example, an evening out for dinner. Even before I leave home if I begin to wonder how expensive it will be, whether I should bother to go, since it is so much trouble to dress, and if I tell myself that cooking my own food definitely tastes better than anything I can possibly get in a restaurant, that I had better stay home, then my evening is ruined before I have started. Just the very pessimism of my thinking in that fashion has spoiled the evening. No matter how good the service would be or how tasty the food was, my appreciation would not be there. It was stifled much before it had a chance to manifest itself.

I have learned to channel my thinking to positive thoughts about everything in general from the most menial tasks to the finest function I may be called on to attend. When I can learn to anticipate a little something in everything I may have to do, or be required to do, amazingly enough it suddenly has some glow and excitement to it, because I thought of it just that way. Life is so beautiful and we have such a very little while to enjoy its beauties, that you literally desecrate it when you indulge in negative thinking. In conclusion, I have learned this one thing: *As a different person, I now reach out, think happy thoughts and wonder each day what treasures are in store for me because I dared and tried.*

We would like to suggest that you read Mrs. Lane's personal testimony of how self-hypnosis helped her. Read it once a day for two weeks. It will serve as a form of inspirational self-therapy.

**Self-hypnotic suggestions
for banishing the "blues"**

Here are some thought-suggestions that you can give yourself during self-hypnosis which will help you combat moods of depression:

1. When I am in one of my melancholy moods I will make sure not to project my disturbed feelings of gloomy disposition onto others.

2. I am going to refuse to indulge in self-pity. Feeling sorry for myself only makes matters worse.

3. I am going to devote time to studying the reasons for my mood-swings.

4. I am going to stop brooding because I'm depressed. I am going to remind myself that depressed spells quite often vanish —that they are *transient* and that everyone at times experiences the "blues" or low moods.

5. I am going to whet my sense of humor whenever I feel low. I am not going to take myself or my problems more seriously than they deserve.

6. I am not going to make worry a *habit*—knowing that 90 per cent of the things we worry about never happen.

7. I am going to stop living in the past. I am not going to feel guilty about something I can't change—it's a waste of mental energy. I am going to learn to forgive myself for past mistakes and live in the present—looking forward to a better tomorrow.

8. I am going to keep myself busy and utilize my leisure time to advantage. I will always find something recreational to do that will give me a lift, like seeing a good movie, reading an interesting book, listening to music or anything that will help me relax aand make me forget my troubles.

9. If my depression is chronic or too deep-seated, I will contact my physician, have him check me physically and will let him decide whether I should consult some specialist.

Points to remember

1. There are two types of depression:
   a. Normal depression (temporary) which everyone experiences at times.

b. Morbid depression (chronic) which is generally associated with physical or mental illness.

2. Analyze your unhappy moods. Understanding them makes it easier for you to combat them.

3. You can find and correct the cause of your unhappiness, utilizing *self-hypnotic techniques.*

4. The important thing is to do *something about your depressed moods,* as suggested in this chapter.

Chapter Eleven

How to create
for yourself
a new personality
and a happier life

●━━━━━━━━━━━━━━━━━━━━━━━━━━━━━●

Just what is meant by "personality"?

▲ Personality is the outward or surface expression of your inner self—your inner you. It represents a medium of communication. It includes a combination of many things—the way you walk, dress, eat and talk, your tone of voice, facial expression, what you say, how you say it, your habit-ways of doing things, mannerisms, the way you express or control your different emotions, your attitude about yourself and others, your desires, dreams and ambitions, your basic attitude toward life, your likes and dislikes, what you believe and disbelieve, your ability to love and be loved, your capacity to survive misfortune. All of these things and others constitute your *total you*. Personality is your *ego-being*. It is equivalent to the skeletal framework or structure of your body. When your *ego* collapses you are unable to function adequately. Your ego needs constant support in order to survive. It is responsible for your reaction to your past experiences, your present mode of living and your hopes for the future.

144

Try to understand
what made you what you are

At this very moment you the reader are what you are because of a sum total of habit-conditioning influences that helped shape your personality from the day you were born—influences which stemmed from your grandparents and parents, brothers, sisters, relatives and friends—influences within the home and outside the home, religious influences, the influence of society, the kind of community in which you were brought up (rural or urban), and your many personal past experiences. Just as it takes a variety of colors to make a rainbow, there are many factors that go to make up each personality. No two human beings are exactly alike in everything.

Fortunately, personality traits are not *inherited*. They are expressions of the inner you, which you have *learned* and *acquired* through *conditioning* and *imitation*.

Your personality is influenced by conscious and unconscious factors. Psychoanalysts believe that you can change your personality only by bringing that which is buried in the subconscious mind to the level of conscious awareness. They try to assist you to develop self-insight.

However, with *self-hypnosis* you can accomplish this very same thing. Through hypnotic autoanalysis you can uncover the hidden factors in your family background and childhood and evaluate them in terms of their influence on your personality-development. You can resolve guilt complexes which have warped your personality. Using autotherapy (posthypnotic suggestion) you can learn to control your emotions. Personality-maturity involves self-control. To develop and maintain a healthy personality you have to keep working at it consistently by suggesting to yourself during self-hypnotic sessions the personality qualities you wish to acquire. You must begin by changing your attitude toward yourself—you have to stop thinking that you are inadequate.

Gradually a definite personality change will emerge from this influence to your subconscious mind. It will happen despite yourself. You will begin to shed your overbearing personality, overcome shyness, become more communicative or conquer any other specific personality problem you may have.

Can you change your personality?

Yes, today many charm and personality development schools are successfully changing people's personalities. It is evidence that you too can change your inner you and become the person you want to be.

You can't make yourself taller but you can develop a *better* personality.

Gordon Allport, psychologist of Harvard, claims personality involves the interaction of three factors: (1) Habits, (2) Traits, (3) Attitudes.

A *habit* is something one does over and over again.

A *trait* is a tendency to do something repeatedly in a similar way. For example, a person may have a trait of being untidy.

An *attitude* is a way of looking at something—life, love, marriage.

Habits, traits and attitudes are *not* inherited. They are learned and acquired. Psychologists know that they can be altered. Undesirable habits can be unlearned. You can develop new habits, new traits and new attitudes using techniques of self-hypnosis. Self-hypnosis can change your appearance, your way of thinking and living.

Many people we know seem not to have changed over the years because they harbor the fallacious idea that you are what you are because of factors in your life that are "fixed." It explains why we often say, "He's a chip off the old block," or "Once a neurotic, always a neurotic."

To change for the better you must be convinced beyond all

doubt that you *can* change: that you can learn to become less hostile, antagonistic and aggressive and overcome emotional handicaps. This conviction must be your starting point in your self-improvement program. It takes knowledge of this fact plus determination and application of what we are going to teach you.

Thomas J. Fleming, in an article called "How to Change Your Personality" (*Cosmopolitan* magazine, July 1961), tells how John F. Kennedy "in his undergraduate days at Harvard was a rather introverted, studious young man, whose main ambition in life was to become either a writer or a teacher." He made a dramatic transformation of personality after he decided to enter politics. According to Fleming, "He overcame his fears and hesitations about public speaking."

He developed an extrovert personality which proved a tremendous advantage to him in meeting people.

You must *want* to change. Many individuals have no incentive to improve themselves only because they were born into a neurotic home and were exposed to the incompatibility of unhappy parents. Or they feel trapped in an unhappy marriage. They take a "What's the use?" attitude. They have self-defeating personalities. You must want to change for your own sake, rather than to please someone else. It is equivalent to keeping clean for your own sake. The wife who becomes fat and blames her obesity on the fact that she is unhappily married is neurotic and searching for alibis to excuse her own immaturity.

Likewise not to improve because you feel it won't be appreciated by someone else is fatal to growth and progress. You reward yourself through accomplishments. You develop a sense of pride, a feeling of worthwhileness and self-satisfaction that enables you to face the future with increasing self-confidence.

No one denies that there is an advantage to having someone encourage you—someone who loves you and has a genuine desire to help you make progress in life. If you have such an advantage it will naturally make it easier for you to attain your individual goals in life. The point we are trying to make is that we do not necessarily need this outside encouragment to bring about self-improvement. No one can stand in your way as you climb in life, if you are determined to concentrate on changing and improving yourself from day to day.

It should be easy for you to effect a transformation of personality and become the kind of person you want to be if you put into practice the suggestions we are about to give you.

The self-hypnosis approach to personality change

You can definitely achieve a better personality with self-hypnosis. You don't have to accept yourself as you are unless you consider yourself to be a mature, normal, well-adjusted person. Self-hypnosis can change your inner you for the better. It can help you develop a magnetic personality.

A person with a magnetic personality is one who has developed the ability of holding his listener spellbound, as it were, of captivating his audience, of enchanting a group of people with his storytelling. This skill of establishing a quick favorable rapport with the person you are talking to can be cultivated.

We all prefer to be around people who are relaxed. Relaxation is contagious. We feel uneasy listening to a nervous speaker because of what psychiatrists call "empathy." We *identify* ourselves with someone who manifests self-consciousness and we become nervous and self-conscious ourselves. On the contrary, the person who is poised and confident makes you feel comfortable. Every time he laughs, you laugh. This magnetic power of a speaker to put his listener in a hypnotic state, hold his attention and convince him of what he's trying to put across, is common to successful public speakers. The late President Roosevelt possessed this power. It has been told that some of the Republican Senators didn't trust themselves listening to him because they felt themselves yielding or drawn to his political views. His manner of talking during his informal "Fireside Chats"—"My . . . friends," etc. We know, for example, candidates for public office who had excellent qualifications, yet whenever they addressed the masses were unable to reach the average man. They talked over his head, as the expression goes. With all due respect to their integrity, sincerity and other fine qualifications, they had never developed the art of expressing themselves in common, everyday language, of making themselves *loved* by everyone in their manner of talking, facial expression or other gestures which would tend to emanate humility, confidence and hope. There are many who are convinced that it was President Eisenhower's *popularity* and *likability* that paved his path to the White House. He had been the people's *hero* during the war. Despite the fact that he was never a Senator or a Congressman, but a military man, he was still elected overwhelmingly as President of the United States.

There are numerous examples of others who possess this innate hypnotic or magnetic appeal. It comes natural to them. It is part of their make-up. Billy Graham is apparently endowed with this persuasive power. But we cannot all be Roosevelts, Eisenhowers or Billy Grahams, gifted with magnetic personalities. Most of us have to learn and teach ourselves the technique of acquiring personality-appeal.

How to acquire personality-magnetism

Start by autosuggesting the idea that you are going to become a very *attentive listener*. This invariably flatters the ego of the person talking to you. Try not to interrupt. If you absolutely have to interrupt, preface your remark with "Do you mind if I interrupt for a moment?" Then go ahead and make your point. We all like to feel important. We are all *ego-hungry*. We like to be listened to. As you listen, look the person in the eyes. Don't wander off or appear distracted because it gives the other person the impression that you aren't interested. He concludes that what he is saying is not too important to you.

David J. Schwartz, author of *The Magic of Thinking Big*, made this interesting observation:

> In hundreds of interviews with people at all levels, I've made this discovery: The bigger the person, the more apt he is to encourage you to talk; the smaller the person, the more apt he is to preach to you.
> Big people monopolize the listening.
> Small people monopolize the talking.

Let self-hypnosis convert you to becoming a good listener. Resolve that you are going to listen attentively and manifest interest in what the other person is saying by asking an occasional question.

Keep your gaze focused on the person talking to you. This establishes rapport between you and the other person.

An eminent professor of psychiatry was once asked, "What makes a good psychiatrist?" He quickly responded: "One who has learned to become a good listener." Patients like to feel that you are genuinely interested in wanting to hear all about their personal problems.

The same professor was asked, "What other quality makes a good psychiatrist?"—to which he replied, "Make each patient love you." By love, of course, he meant letting the patient develop a respect, a confidence in your integrity. He added, "Become sympathetic. If you must be firm, be kind. Don't scold. Educate instead. Don't tell a patient about the stupidity of his past mistakes. Tell him what you think he is capable of accomplishing. Inspire hope. Conveying the impression that you are condemning him for his wrongs is only adding to his frustrations. A patient comes to you to be encouraged, not to be admonished."

Psychoanalysts use the term "positive transference" to refer to the establishment of a favorable rapport with their patients.

A good doctor-patient relationship is essential to a patient's recovery.

A good interpersonal relationship between you and another individual or a group is also essential to your success in life. You have to make a conscious effort to make other people believe in you, believe in what you think and say.

Give yourself the posthypnotic suggestion that you are going to think before you speak, being careful not to offend anyone, that you are going to give people the feeling that you are sincere and a warm person. Practice being simple in your language so that you are understood. After all, speech is a form of communication. If very few people understand what you're driving at, your efforts will prove futile. It is equivalent to receiving a letter from someone whose handwriting is so illegible that you can't make it out.

While you're at it, learn to improve your vocabulary

One specific way of improving your personality is to develop the ability to communicate with people. Words are to a writer what nails are to a carpenter. When we possess a good vocabulary we become confident in expressing ourselves. People are impressed whenever we manifest a clever choice of words. It reflects an educated mind. We all like to listen to conversation that is stimulating.

You don't have to be a college graduate to have a good vocabulary. Anyone can learn the meaning of new words. It merely requires the price of a dictionary, the energy to look up the meaning of a word and the ability to use it properly in conversation or in a letter to a friend.

Wilfred Funk and Norman Lewis, authors of 30 *Days to a More Powerful Vocabulary*, claim that the vocabulary of the average person practically stops growing by the middle twenties. Consequently, they recommend that you need a plan for increasing your vocabulary if you expect progress to be made.

Regarding the importance of building up a good vocabulary in relation to achieving success in life the above-mentioned authors make the following significant statements:

If your vocabulary is limited, your chances of success are limited.

It has been discovered that the most common characteristics of outstanding success is "an extensive knowledge of the exact meaning of English words."

One of the easiest and quickest ways to get ahead is by consciously building up your knowledge of words.

The extent of your vocabulary indicates the degree of your intelligence. Your brain power will increase as you learn to know more words.

Words are your tools of thought. You can't even think at all without them.

Your words are your keys for your thoughts. And the more words you have at your command the deeper, clearer and more accurate will be your thinking.

A command of English will not only improve the processes of your mind. It will give you assurance, build your self-confidence, lend color to your personality, increase your popularity. Your words are your personality. Your vocabulary is you.

Words can also change the direction of your life. They have often raised a man from mediocrity to success.*

Steps for improving your vocabulary

1. Get yourself a pocket notebook and begin jotting down new words and their meaning. Number them. Learn 500 to a thousand words that you intend to practice using.

2. During a daily session of self-hypnosis repeat out loud to yourself 10 new words you have looked up. Your subconscious mind will absorb their meaning.

* Reprinted from *30 Days to a More Powerful Vocabulary* by Wilfred Funk and Norman Lewis, by permission of the Publisher, Wilfred Funk. Inc.

3. Give yourself the suggestion that you are going to carry your notebook wherever you go. Take advantage of every opportunity you get to refer to your list of words so that you have their meanings completely memorized.

4. Make a game of this special vocabulary training. Make it fun. Look forward to learning the meaning of a new word. Study the derivation of each word.

5. Make the increasing of your vocabulary a *habit*. Acquire the habit as you would any other habit, using techniques of self-hypnosis.

You will be surprised how soon you will be able to express yourself fluently. You will begin to radiate confidence in your speech. You will be complimented by your friends. All in all, you will be pleased with your ability to talk to people with a feeling of ease.

Develop a tolerant personality with self-hypnosis

Remind yourself that the world does not belong to any one race. The stars, the oceans, the moon, the mountains and rivers belong to no one. Everything man acquires he leaves behind. It is also important to remind yourself how humble we should be. If a photographer were to intermingle the adult population of the world and have every human being stand elbow to elbow for a single group picture (assuming that it could be done), can you imagine how long it would take for anyone, whether he were a king or queen, millionaire or truck driver, to find himself in a rolled-up photograph of two and a half billion human beings? This should give you some idea of how insignificant we really are. When we speak of the world in terms of millions of years, you can appreciate how it compares to the average span of man's life—our threescore and ten years are only a grain of sand on the beach of life. It takes this kind of reality and humility to appreciate, *tolerate*, and respect the rights of *all* people as human beings. Progress cannot exist without successful interpersonal relationships. Our world should be one of sharing—a sharing of material things as well as ideals.

The point of it all is that we need to assume a proper attitude about people in general before we can learn self-hypnotic techniques for getting along with the people we come in contact with. To become *tolerant* of people you must love life—you must like yourself and your surrounding world.

During a self-hypnotic session suggest the idea that tolerance is one of the major personality assets of a healthy normal person. Tell yourself that people will get under your skin, to use a common expression, only if you let them. Anyone can get along with a mature individual. The real challenge and test of maturity is to learn to get along with people who are difficult and unhappy. Everyone has to deal with hard-to-get-along-with people, whether they like it or not.

A rule to follow and one to include under autosuggestion is to repeat each day, "I am not going to let myself imitate the undesirable personality traits of other people."

Enlist the cooperation of your friends for personality-improvement

Let your friends know that you are trying to improve your personality. Ask them to be frank with you. Have them tell you what they think your faults are. After all, they have had the opportunity of observing you over the years. Assure them beforehand that you are not going to be oversensitive and resent their honest critical evaluation of you. You can learn much about yourself by enlisting the opinions and advice of your friends. Ask them for suggestions as to what they think you can do to improve yourself. In the long run they will admire and respect you for your willingness to change.

In doing this, be prepared to *accept* whatever advice you are given that you regard as constructive.

▲ *Alice Acquires a New Personality Through Self-Hypnosis.*
Alice had been an introvert practically all of her life. Her parents
had died when she was a child. Brought up by an aunt who was
strict, she developed a deep sense of inferiority early in life. Her
aunt made all of her decisions for her. As a consequence when
she grew up she manifested a complete lack of confidence. Although she managed to support herself as a typist-clerk she never
achieved enough maturity to establish a normal adjustment to
the opposite sex or to people in general. She attributes this gap
in her life to extreme shyness. She refused social invitations because she was too self-conscious to participate in a friendly conversation with anyone. Even at church functions she seldom
spoke to someone else she knew. She was aware of the fact that
her loneliness in life was caused by her own refusal to make
friends. When she could no longer "go on," to use her own words,
when she was getting more and more "depressed," she decided
to seek help. She had been wallowing in self-pity.

Alice was taught the techniques of self-hypnosis as outlined
in Chapter Two. She began using it around people. She also
learned how to use self-suggestion to advantage. She told herself,
after being able to induce her own hypnotic state, that she would
make herself become more communicative. She practiced smiling
more and made herself go out more to the theatre, to someone's
home, to a concert. By doing more talking, becoming more
friendly, she gradually began to come out of her shell.

Self-hypnosis enabled her to make plans. She told herself
she would take a trip to Europe, which became a reality. Her
friends tell her about the remarkable change in her personality.
She tells them that she finally awakened to the realization that
she had the capacity to overcome her shyness—that through self-
hypnosis she was able to develop a feeling of self-confidence.
Her voice even changed. At one time it was weak and child-like
in quality. Now she speaks in a more assertive manner. She
learned to gesticulate and vary her voice-tone and observed that
she was able to hold her listener's attention. She looked differ-

ently because she felt differently inside. Alice claims she can always rely on a session or two of self-hypnosis to carry her through any trying or challenging situation. She takes pride in having developed an extroverted type of personality and is no longer handicapped by her shyness.

Here are some of the things that we taught Alice to repeat to herself during her self-hypnosis sessions:

1. I must tell myself that tension causes nervousness. Nervousness causes a lack of confidence, and a lack of confidence causes shyness. If I practice the art of self-relaxation, using the method of self-hypnosis I will overcome tension. If I learn to become less tense I will develop greater poise and in turn will gain greater self-confidence. To conquer self-consciousness I must conquer tension. This I can accomplish by mastering the art of self-hypnosis.

2. I am going to find consolation in the fact that over half of the adult population suffers from some form of self-consciousness or experiences some degree of embarrassment in social relations. Therefore I am not alone in my battle against shyness.

3. I must not consider shyness as something to be ashamed of. Shyness is merely a symptom of a lack of self-confidence, feelings of insecurity, inferiority and a fear of people.

4. I am going to accept the conclusions of psychologists that self-consciousness is the result of self-centeredness, thinking more about myself and the kind of impression I make rather than what I am trying to say or do that will benefit others.

5. The best way not to feel inferior to others is to do something about my inferiority complex. Confidence follows accomplishment. Feeling sorry for myself will never cure me of my shyness. Working hard, making myself useful, doing something for someone else will give me the kind of inner satisfaction that brings with it a feeling of self-confidence.

6. I must not use my sense of inferiority as an alibi for being too lazy to improve myself.

7. I am going to use the technique of self-hypnosis to develop a will to improve, a desire to study, learn and make progress in every aspect of my life.

8. If I improve my appearance, I will experience a more comfortable feeling when I am around people.

9. I am going to give myself the daily suggestion that I will talk more to people, act more friendly and initiate the kind of conversation that will enlist the interest of the other person.

10. Through self-hypnosis I will overcome my fear of people by suggesting to myself that I have nothing to fear, that if I am kind, considerate and sincere, people will accept me for these qualities.

Self-hypnosis improves your memory and ability to learn

Ralph Daigh, a writer, reports how a young man in his final year of medical school at an eastern university told him how he had been using self-hypnosis throughout his undergraduate and postgraduate days, for the most part with the full knowledge of his professors. Daigh informs us that "He made Phi Beta Kappa, has the highest grades in his class at medical school and was offered possibly the highest salary ever offered an intern to stay at the school's hospital for several years of hypnotic research." This young man, so Daigh tells us, is the son of a professional hypnotist and his grandfather was both a physician and a hypnotist.

Hypnosis and its application in the field of education is also reported by Ann Cutler (*The American Weekly*, January 1, 1960):

> The field of education is one where hypnosis will undoubtedly play a more important role as its benefits become recognized. Experiments indicate that hypnosis helps increase comprehension, aids retention, speed of learning and general efficiency. In addition, hypnosis supplies the motivation to learn the consequent pleasure in performance.

Dr. Linn F. Cooper of Washington, D.C., found that David W. Rodgin, a graduate student in psychology at Purdue was able to master a standard learning experiment in only 7.4 seconds that it had taken him four times as long to learn while awake. Tested after 24 hours he retained more of what he learned under hypnosis and could relearn the forgotten matter in less time.

Linda Darnell, screen actress, faced with the learning of a large part for the play "Late Love," which was to open in Chicago, felt she could not possibly memorize the role in time. Frantically, she phoned her doctor-hypnotist in Los Angeles. He flew to Chicago and "placed her in such a state of relaxation and receptivity" that she was able to learn the part letter perfect in only two sessions. Miss Darnell opened to rave notices.

Summary

1. Personality is your inner you—your total you. It's a combination of everything that makes you what you are.

2. Personality traits are *not* inherited. They are learned and acquired through *conditioning* and *imitation*.

3. Self-hypnosis can help you develop a new and better personality—a magnetic personality—one that enables you to get along with everyone.

4. Accept the helpful criticism of your friends, using self-hypnosis to purge yourself of whatever personality shortcomings you possess.

Continued on page 18

Explanatory footnotes

Sales figures are unofficial.

u—Indicates a new 52-week high. d—Indicates a new 52-week low.

s—Stock split or stock dividend amounting to 25 per cent or more in the past 52 weeks. The high-low range and dividend begin with the date of split or stock dividend, and do not cover the entire 52-week period.

n—New issue for the past 52 weeks. The high-low range begins with the start of trade in the new issue and goes to cover the entire 52-week period.

Unless otherwise noted, rates of dividends in the foregoing table are annual disbursements based on the last quarterly or semi-annual declaration. Special or extra dividends or payments not designated as regular are identified in the following footnotes.

a—Also extra or extras. b—Annual rate plus stock dividend. c—Liquidating dividend. e—Declared or paid in preceding 12 months. i—Declared or paid after stock dividend or split up. j—Paid this year, dividend omitted, deferred or no action taken at last dividend meeting. k—Declared or paid this year, an accumulative issue with dividends in arrears. r—Declared or paid in preceding 12 months plus stock dividend. t—Paid in stock in preceding 12 months, estimated cash value on ex-dividend or ex-distribution date.

x—Ex-dividend or ex-rights. y—Ex-dividend and sales in full. z—Sales in full.

cld—Called. wd—When distributed. wi—When issued. ww—With warrants. xw—Without warrants. xdis—Ex-distribution.

vj—In bankruptcy or receivership or being reorganized under the Bankruptcy Act, or securities assumed by such companies.

g—Dividends and earnings in Canadian money. No yield or PE is shown because the stock trades in U.S. dollars.

Chapter Twelve

How to achieve
hypnotic power, control,
and influence over others

Repeat during self-hypnosis that people are bound to like me if—

1. I am kind and unselfish.
2. I am willing to do favors when I can.
3. I smile more.
4. I listen well.
5. I make conversation interesting.
6. I avoid sarcasm.
7. I exercise tolerance.
8. I control my emotions.
9. I try to be courteous and polite.
10. I am sincere and try to be myself.
11. I think before I speak.
12. I avoid being overcritical.
13. I try to understand why people behave as they do.

14. I act friendly and cheerful.
15. I compliment people for the things that deserve praising.
16. I don't exploit people.
17. I make other people feel important.
18. I learn to mind my own business.
19. I stop needless complaining.
20. I radiate enthusiasm.

What getting along with people
by using self-hypnosis can do for you

1. *Bring you greater success in your job or career.*

According to Lee Giblin, author of a recently published book *How to Have Confidence and Power in Dealing with People* (Prentice-Hall, Inc., 1956), "The Carnegie Institute of Technology analyzed the records of 10,000 persons and arrived at the conclusion that 15 per cent of success is due to technical training, to brains and skills on the job and 85 per cent of success is due to personality factors in the ability to deal with people successfully."

He also informs us that "When the Bureau of Vocations Guidance at Harvard University made a study of thousands of men and women who had been fired they found that for every one person who lost his job for failure to do the work, two persons lost their job for failure to deal successfully with people."

Giblin concludes that "66 per cent of all failures in the business world are failures in human relations—that so-called personality problems, such as timidity, shyness and self-consciousness are basically problems in dealing with people."

2. *Provide opportunities for other people to help you.*

An executive or boss is more apt to help someone he likes than someone he dislikes. When you make friends easily, you become popular. Persons who are popular are usually extroverts. They are entertaining. They like to make other people happy. They enjoy life more and as a result of making numerous friends, they capitalize on their contacts to advance themselves. They have learned that it doesn't pay to be shy, that it is normal to ask favors, and to know what you want out of life. More people are willing to help you than you realize if you have earned the right to ask for their help.

3. *Give yourself opportunities to help others.*

Happiness in part comes to you when you make other people happy. People like you if you show them that you are unselfish. Happiness includes giving, receiving and sharing. We are all dependent on one another for happiness. You can make people happy. They can make you happy. If you make it your business to get along with people you will experience an inner contentment, self-satisfaction, a feeling of accomplishment. Look for ways of helping others—they can be found.

4. *Increase your self-confidence and self-esteem.*

If you know others like you, you are bound to be proud of yourself. You become less shy. You get to like making new friends. You begin to develop the techniques of feeling at ease in the presence of others and putting others at ease. You are no longer frightened by people. You discover that the secret of making friends is to act friendly and cheerful. People will accept you if you're sincere and manifest a genuine wish to be a friend.

When you are using self-hypnosis keep the following in mind

If someone is sarcastic, don't go him one better and answer him in even a more sarcastic manner. If someone insults you, don't insult him back, even if it would be very easy to do so. In the long run the other person will admire your self-control. He will respect you and after he has had time to cool off he may surprise you with an apology. If you don't think so, try it sometime. Find out for yourself. Once you have discovered the wisdom of this advice you'll find that it's rather a simple matter —getting along with people whether they are congenial or not.

Life will become easier for you. You'll decide not to take people too seriously.

Hating certain people will never solve anything. Don't let someone else's hate feelings rub off on you. You can help and influence people who seem obnoxious or self-centered by setting an example. Try to teach the person who hates that it is better to love than to hate. Handle him with firmness and kindness. Remind yourself that a person who is difficult is generally one who has never learned to get along with himself. That's the reason he can't get along with others.

Don't worry about having to impress people. Use self-hypnosis to help yourself adopt a relaxed attitude. Be your real "you." It's the secret of feeling at ease around people.

Self-hypnosis enhances salesmanship ability

Manufacturers have long recognized the tremendous value in publicizing and advertising their products. The public is influenced by the cleverness and attractiveness of advertisements. As we have said many times in this book, our minds are influenced by what we think, what we hear and what we see. You have often heard someone say, "I couldn't resist buying it." It's not always the product that counts; it's how it's described and promoted. *Hypnotic appeal* plays an important role in the field of selling and advertising. People must be made to *want* to buy a particular product. Publishers are aware of this. The mail-order brochure must be so worded that the individual is made to feel that he *needs* the book that is being advertised, that it will have tremendous value for him, that he will benefit in many spheres from the content of the book. That's why titles of books are so important. They must be provocative. The reader's curiosity must be aroused. Paperback covers try to quickly capture your attention, via sensational titles and sexy pictures of semi-clad women. This "visual appeal" which we have talked about comes under the category of "hypnotic equivalents."

Every salesman knows the value of the so-called indirect approach. He attempts to sell himself before he mentions his product. He uses a "let's get acquainted" approach. If he knows you like fishing, he may start by telling you of the fish he caught on his last fishing trip. If he discovers you're a golfer, the conversation centers around golf, etc. In other words, he wants you to like him as a person. He tries to find something he has in common with you. You recall that in courtship the man attempts to make the girl fall in love with him. When the girl finds herself married, she exclaims later, "He swept me off my feet. I was irresistibly attracted to him." The same thing applies in the field of selling. Self-hypnosis can give one the kind of personality that will increase his ability to sell.

For example, a salesman must not appear overanxious or tense. He must be soft-spoken. He must radiate confidence in himself as well as in his product. He must first relax himself before he approaches his prospective client. He should acquaint himself with some basic elementary rules of applied psychology. To talk enough and not too much is a simple rule to keep in mind. To smile and appear friendly helps establish a proper rapport. Every salesman possesses his own repertoire of funny stories. Dining and wining your client paves the way toward a sale.

Have you ever heard someone say, "I can see why he's a success. He has a wonderful personality." Personality-appeal is really hypnotic-appeal. The salesman with a sense of humor, who emanates poise and relaxation, who doesn't try to "oversell," who is friendly and sincere and can make you feel he is doing you a favor by bringing his product to your attention, has what we call hypnotic-appeal—a persuasive personality.

Let us assume that we have convinced you that in the field of selling and advertising, the customer is actually "hypnotized" into buying a house, a boat or a car, or taking a trip to Europe, subscribing to a magazine or investing in a certain stock. What you want to know now is, "How do I develop this hypnotic power in myself?" Salesmen in particular are interested in learning how they can increase their income by utilizing the techniques of hypnosis and autohypnosis.

If you have studied diligently the instructions that have been given to you in previous chapters, especially the chapter dealing with personality-development, then all you need to do is to make out a list of self-given suggestions, (which are to be repeated in your daily practice sessions of self-hypnosis) along the following lines:

1. I am going to start out every morning with the idea that this is going to be a *good* day for me, that I am going to experience an inner feeling of confidence, a feeling that I can almost sell anything to anyone, that I can make more sales than I ever had before.

2. I believe in the usefulness and value of what I am selling.

3. If I am going to have to deal with people, I must learn to like people and not have them disturb me emotionally.

4. I am going to concentrate on improving and maintaining a good outward appearance in order to create a favorable first impression.

5. I am going to train myself not to do all the talking, but to listen well, to ask questions so that my client is made to feel comfortable and not high-pressured into buying something against his better judgment.

6. I am going to study and analyze each person I talk to and adapt my sales approach to fit his particular personality.

7. I am going to learn to compliment and praise people when praise is justified.

8. I am going to remind myself not to appear overanxious, not to oversell or talk myself out of a sale by becoming obnoxiously persistent or reaching a point of actually annoying the other person.

9. I am going to read and study as many books as I can, per-

taining to the psychology of selling and apply whatever knowledge I acquire.

10. I am going to practice the 4-A's method of self-hypnosis
until I have achieved the self-mastery I need in order to become
more successful and enjoy the luxuries of increased prosperty.

Visual reminders

We believe in recommending *supplementary* methods of
achieving self-improvement goals. Giving yourself messages by
printing something on a card and thumb tacking it on a wall in
your room may help you stick to a given resolution. Everyone can
make use of this system. On the highways you come across signs
like "Stay Alive—Keep Awake" or "Drive Safely—Live Longer."
The sign "Think" actually makes people cautious around dangerous machinery. They are less apt to do something carelessly.
If you are tense and nervous, perhaps it might be well to put a
"Learn to Relax" sign where you can see it every day. It's not
what we know, it's what we forget to do. We need constant
reminders. Everyone knows it's better to be calm and relaxed, but
how many of us remember not to get emotionally upset? As
husbands, wives and parents we forget, and before we realize it
we're in some sort of emotional outburst.

Let's face it. Our minds are influenced by thousands of suggestions in something we see—a sign or a picture. Why not
capitalize on this tendency of every human being to react to
what he sees? We are all receptive and susceptible to "visual
suggestions."

If you are trying to lose weight, have some old pictures of
yourself when you were slender enlarged and look at it every
morning and night. It will serve as an inducement for you to
reduce. It will be a daily reminder.

If you lose your temper at the drop of a hat, print a sign
"Keep Calm" and pin it up where you can see it all day long.

It sounds childish, but what's the difference if it works? When you've achieved what you're after you no longer have to put up signs to look at. You will have developed by then the *habit* of keeping calm.

You often see signs like "Smile" in restaurants. It's surprising what effect this has on both the waitress and the customer. It all comes under the category of "Visual Suggestive Therapy."

Essential points to remember

1. Dealing with people successfully pays dividends.

2. Use self-hypnosis to help you develop personality-qualities that will make people like you. (These are listed at the beginning of this chapter.)

3. Learn to get along with yourself and it will be easier to get along with others.

4. Personality-development is the key to successful relationships with people.

5. Like people and they will like you.

6. Increase your self-esteem and you will be better respected by everyone.

7. When you have mastered the art of self-relaxation, you will be able to put others at ease. People relax and feel comfortable in the presence of those who radiate relaxation.

8. Find some good in everyone.

9. Remind yourself that people respond well to compliments. We all like to be inspired and encouraged.

10. Use techniques of self-hypnosis to increase your tolerance quotient (TQ), and you will never have any trouble getting along with people.

Chapter Thirteen

Self-hypnosis
techniques
to make a success
of your marriage

●━━━━━━━━━━━━━━━━━━━━━━●

▲ Each year more than a million couples marry, and each year every fourth marriage ends in divorce. There is no need for this high divorce rate. Many marriage failures are caused by factors which could be remedied if the couples were convinced that they had the capacity to solve their own problems. If each husband and wife took a personality-inventory of themselves and made a sincere effort through self-analysis and self-discipline to correct their faults, they would improve their marital relationship immeasurably and make divorce unnecessary in many instances.

How to attain greater happiness
in marriage through self-hypnosis

If you were unhappy before marriage, it could well be that subconsciously you are projecting your own inner unhappiness onto your husband or wife.

Ask yourself, "Did I come from an unhappy home? What influence may this fact be having on my marriage?" These and many other questions may help you trace the source of your troubles. Before you can remedy something you must analyze and understand it.

Try soul-searching—look within. Decide what needs to be done, using the techniques of self-hypnosis.

Proceed with autotherapy—doing something about yourself and your problem. The incentive to want to help yourself can be achieved through self-hypnosis.

Subject yourself to daily sessions of autorelaxation, inducing a hypnotic state and repeating daily the insights you have gained and what you intend to do to become a *better husband*, or a *better wife. It will work if you make it work.* Try it.

Get a notebook and write out a list of what it takes to make a marriage successful. We know, for example, that sexual harmony is essential to a happy marriage. Husbands and wives who are sexually unhappy are unable to tolerate little things which two people who are sexually compatible would overlook. When a marriage suffers from sexual disharmony it often takes only some minor conflict to bring about the final break. Arguments and disagreements which would normally be settled quickly and be forgotten take on major proportions. The disagreements are secretly fed and sustained by virulent hostility that results from a frustrating sexual relationship and poisons the marriage. The end result may either be divorce or a half-marriage—marriage in name and appearance, but not in fact.

Self-hypnosis can make you a sexually mature person, as you have learned in Chapter Seven. Develop and accept a more wholesome attitude toward sex and its importance in marriage. The proper attitude means an increased capacity for love. A mature person will not choose to remain a victim of chronic unhappiness caused by sexual disharmony. An intelligent couple will always do something about their sex-unhappiness.

You can acquire knowledge in the basic principles of sexual

harmony by reading various authoritative books on the subject. They contain specific information pertaining to lovemaking techniques. Self-hypnosis will assist you in putting what you have learned into practice—with the result that your marriage will be a happier one.

The following are a few posthypnotic suggestions which we recommend that you use as a guide to enrich your married life.

Memorize and repeat them to yourself daily, during each hypnotic session:

1. In addition to achieving sexual maturity I am going to make myself a lovable person. I must realize that love must be earned. I must be capable of *giving* love. I am going to practice developing a lovable disposition. Making myself lovable is one of the secrets of capturing and holding love.

2. I am going to think carefully before saying anything—being mindful of the effect my words may have on others. I am going to avoid being sarcastic, learn to become more diplomatic and develop the art of friendly and interesting conversation. I am going to be less argumentative. If I learn to control the impulse to say the wrong thing, in haste, I will become a better person, one who will be loved and respected.

3. Each day I shall remind myself to be less sensitive. Love-frustrations are often the result of oversensitivity. We all know couples who truly love each other, yet constantly bicker over trivialities, each oversensitive and on the defensive. Their love is like a duet, played on a discordant note.

4. I am going to make myself a congenial and companionable mate. The art of companionship is a quality that outweighs and outlasts any other consideration in marriage. It is an outgrowth of love. To be companionable I must become tolerant and unselfish. I am going to share this life with my mate with tolerance and humor.

By making each of the above suggestions a daily self-improvement goal which can be attained with a do-it-yoursef determination and self-hypnotic techniques you can make your marriage a lifelong happy experience.

Twelve helpful suggestions for husbands

Here are some things which every husband should tell himself during sessions of self-hypnosis and put into practice if he wishes to achieve a happy and satisfying husband-wife relationship:

1. My wife wishes to be loved and respected as a person.

2. If I make my wife feel emotionally and economically secure, *needed and loved,* she will respond better physically and make a better wife.

3. I must make my wife feel like a *woman* and not a mother-substitute.

4. I must keep reminding myself that to a woman love is the most important thing in her existence.

5. I must give my wife companionship.

6. I must *not* expect my wife to conform to my way of thinking about everything.

7. I must realize that men and women, as sexes, are different —not only anatomically, but in their respective emotional and physical needs.

8. I will make an attempt to understand and appreciate feminine psychology so as to understand better the underlying motivations of my wife's behavior.

9. I cannot expect love and respect from my wife if I belittle or abuse her.

10. My wife expects me to think like a man, feel like a man and act like a man.

11. I must also remind myself that little courtesies, tender attentions and acts of kindness are as important to her as material gifts.

12. It is up to me to teach her to feel unashamed and un-

inhibited in the expression of her natural impulses and have her accept sex as a manifestation of love—the harmonious blending of body and soul.

Twelve helpful suggestions for wives

Here are some things which every wife should believe and tell herself during self-hypnosis sessions:

1. My husband needs to have his ego inflated, which I can do by encouraging and inspiring him.

2. Every husband wants his wife to be a companion—a cooperator, an assistant in his struggle for security and happiness.

3. If I show my husband that I am growing, improving myself and becoming more mature he is bound to respect and love me more.

4. Bickering, fussing, quarreling and nagging are all enemies of marriage-happiness.

5. During one of my sessions of self-hypnosis I am going to remind myself to be more *appreciative* of everything my husband has done toward making me happy and making our marriage a success.

6. There is no reason why I cannot exhibit greater enthusiasm and real interest in his work or professional career.

7. I am going to make every effort to be sexually responsive —not to reject or inhibit him by saying the wrong thing in the wrong way at the wrong time—or doing something that will make him feel disappointed in me.

8. No husband desires to love a woman who is overaggressive —oversensitive—overcritical.

9. I must avoid being the kind of neurotic wife who is suspicious, jealous, overly possessive and emotionally unstable.

10. I am going to practice becoming more tolerant, forgiving and understanding.

11. I will direct my efforts toward making my husband want

to love me by maintaining a cheerful disposition and making myself lovable.

12. I can use self-hypnosis to help me develop a more harmonious personality-relationship between myself and my husband and keep working at it until it becomes a *fact* and not merely a goal.

A marriage that was saved with self-hypnosis

John and Mary were a sexually and emotionally incompatible couple who had come to the mutual conclusion that divorce was the only answer to their difficulties. Their attorney suggested that they both give their marriage a last chance. They had one child, an eight-year-old girl, and they both admitted they wanted to spare her the handicap of a broken home if this was at all possible. Coming face to face with the possibility that they might not have exhausted all efforts to regain their love, they embarked on a program of self-understanding.

The husband decided he was going to adhere to a few self-hypnotic suggestions. Every evening, just before falling asleep, in a state of complete relaxation he devoted five minutes to repeating his plans for improved living and his determination to put them into practice:

1. I shall strive to be a good husband-lover.
2. I shall be considerate, understanding and kind to my wife.
3. I shall interest myself in the welfare of my child—seeking ways to give her love and providing her with opportunities for love and responsibilities.

His wife made her own list of things she was going to tell herself to do. She labeled them "Things I Am Responsible For." Here they are:

1. I am responsible for giving and being able to receive happiness in physical relations with my husband.

2. I am responsible for keeping myself physically attractive, clean and desirable for my husband.

3. I am responsible for giving him the greatest happiness of which I am capable.

4. As a wife, I am responsible for a neat orderly home for my husband.

5. I shall value my husband as the provider of food, clothing, shelter, luxuries and pleasures. I shall be considerate and understanding of his problems. I shall be kind to him. I shall love him.

6. It is my responsibility to teach my child, by example, what real love is and how to work out his problems intelligently, instead of emotionally, how he can live with the greatest amount of happiness in this society of ours.

This couple is experiencing renewed happiness in their marriage only because they learned the wisdom of helping themselves with techniques of self-therapy.

Self-hypnosis can also make you a better parent

Our central theme throughout the book has been that YOU are capable of accomplishing anything—within reason—that you set your mind to. *It is all up to you.* However, you must first plant the seed of confidence—that you can achieve your goal—in your own mind. You must allow this seed—"I want to, I must, I can, I will"—grow and develop in your subconscious mind. It must permeate your everyday thinking. You will then be ready to use your 4-A's method of autohypnosis to accomplish your objective.

Let us assume that you have decided to become a better parent. You want self-hypnosis to do this for you. You start with the conviction that your goal is an *attainable* one—that it *can* be done. We can only achieve in life that which is possible. Becoming a better parent is certainly possible.

Utilizing the 4-A's method of self-hypnosis (autorelaxation, autosuggestion, autoanalysis and autotherapy), you proceed in the direction of your goal. You begin by making your mind receptive to self-analysis, using the technique of autorelaxation which, as you have been taught, prepares your mind to *think out* your problem.

During self-hypnosis ask yourself questions pertaining specifically to what you are trying to achieve. Questions like: "What does becoming a good parent consist of?" "What personality traits do I have which interfere with my being a good parent?" "How did I acquire these destructive elements in my personality?" "Are my children a problem only because I have never been able to understand or control my own emotions?" "Why do I react the way I do toward my children?" "Am I unhappily married and taking it out on the children?" "Am I disappointed in myself and making my children the scapegoat victims of my own frustrations?" "Do I expect too much from my children?" "Am I too strict?" "Do I give them the required amount of love, affection and encouragement?" "Do I have a tendency to blame them when I really should be blaming myself?"

Only in this way can you get to the bottom of your problem with your children. One psychiatrist-writer concluded that there are no problem children, there are only problem parents.

Let us say you have found the answers to all of your questions. You ask, "What do I do now?"

Now you proceed with Step 4, namely *autotherapy*. Having completed your self-analysis you plant thought-ideas in your mind (posthypnotic suggestions). You can think them silently, if you wish or repeat them aloud. It is essential of course that you believe everything you tell yourself. Suggest that when you open your eyes and come out of your hypnotic state, you are going to begin to put into effect these self-given suggestions. They will soon become part of your new self. You are now on your way toward becoming a better parent.

1. *I am going to stop shouting at my children.*

Parents who raise their voices and become easily angered are guilty of contributing toward the development of neuroticism in their children. Children who are shouted at soon learn to shout back. Shouting has a tendency to make children "nervous."

2. *I am never going to bicker or quarrel with my husband or wife in the presence of my children.*

Children are oversensitive. They react adversely to parental incompatibility. If they sense that their parents aren't happy, they begin to feel insecure, and develop various kinds of psychosomatic ailments. They may become shy, belligerent or antisocial. Parents should spare their children anything that will tend to disillusion them or make them unhappy. Instead they should try to create and maintain a happy home environment for them.

3. *I am going to avoid being unfair or inconsistent in the management of my children.*

Many parents either pamper their children by being oversolicitous and catering to their every whim and wish, or they become strict disciplinarians, causing their children to feel constantly frustrated. It is far wiser to avoid extremes—to be firm but kind. You cannot hope to have your children grow up to be well-adjusted adults if you are forever scolding them or favoring one over the other. *Educating* them into better behavior is a more intelligent approach.

4. *As a father I am going to convince myself that it is very important that I establish a close relationship between myself and my children.*

Being a good father means more than just being a good provider. It means taking time out to talk to your children, share their pleasures and give them a secure sense of being loved and protected. Children need the affection and companionship of their father as much as they need the love of their mother. They need *bi-parental* love.

5. *I am going to make a sincere effort to help my children achieve self-confidence and emotional maturity.*

Parents quite often expect too much from their children. They feel that they own them. They become possessive and often refuse to allow a child to do independent thinking. Children who become too dependent on their parents, so-called "family-slaves," grow up to fear responsibility. Most children respond to fair treatment.

We admit that to be a good parent these days is not easy. You have to work at it every day. If you feel you need added help, why not consult a counselor, or read books written especially for parents or articles devoted to parent-child problems? Make becoming a good parent as important as anything else in your life. There is nothing more rewarding than the satisfaction of knowing that you have done a good job of giving your children a good start—that you have taught them to be self-sufficient, mature and law-abiding. Better children will mean fewer divorces, and happier marriages. Better children result in better citizens and better citizens make better nations—a stepping-stone in the direction of a better world.

Summary

1. Using techniques of self-hypnosis, you can become a more compatible marital partner.

2. You have just learned that there are certain specific rules (self-given suggestions) you can use as a guide that will result in a better husband-wife relationship.

3. Marriage can become a *lifelong happy experience* if you are willing to *work* at it.

4. Self-hypnosis can definitely increase your capacity for *new happiness in marriage* and make you a better parent.

5. Before running impulsively to a divorce lawyer consult a reputable marriage-counselor. Self-hypnotic techniques will help you respond more successfully to professional guidance.

Chapter Fourteen

Using hypnotic magic
to stay young
and live longer

You are as old as you feel

▲ To expect self-hypnosis to be successful in helping you to stay young longer and enjoy happier living, there are many things you must know about the problem of growing old gracefully.

For one thing you should convince yourself that there exists a great deal of literal truth in the proverbial expression, "You are as old as you feel."

Dr. Wilhelm Stekel, one of the original collaborators with Professor Sigmund Freud in the field of psychoanalysis, once wrote that age is a relative factor—that some men of 30 feel like men of 60 and, vice versa, men in the calendar age of 60 not uncommonly feel as though they are still in their thirties. He concluded there was only one true means of rejuvenation: keeping your heart everlastingly young, being able to burn spiritually for ideals, for all that is beautiful in this world and for all that can thrill you emotionally.

Make happier living your goal

No one wishes to prolong life for the mere attainment of old age. We want to live longer only if we can make the harvest years of our life both healthful and enjoyable. We want to know how we can keep young in spirit.

One of the first requirements for achieving successful results with self-hypnosis insofar as growing old gracefully is concerned is to accept the self-given suggestion that "I am not necessarily as old as my arteries, but rather I am as old as I feel." This should be your key formula for staying young.

By achieving serenity of mind through techniques of self-hypnosis you will be adding years to your life. In previous chapters we gave you specific suggestions as to how you can conquer fear, eliminate tension and master the art of relaxation. This in itself will aid you in experiencing peace of mind during the autumn years of your life.

If you have learned to use self-hypnosis to improve your living habits, to give you better health, then you can expect to add a number of years—possibly an extra decade—to your normal life expectancy. But as we pointed out, your goal should be not to merely live longer, but to have a richer, happier life. After all, there is not much point in lingering on in a vale of tears and tribulations. Unless the later years can be full of zest, interest and meaning, they are scarcely worth the effort required to keep the dull embers of life from extinction. Who cares to live unless he can LIVE.

A theory of aging: mind over body

There are many theories and explanations as to why we grow old, why some of us grow old prematurely, why others develop symptoms of senile thinking. There are those who never seem to grow old, while some curtail their span of life because of having lost their will to live.

Personally, we are inclined to the opinion that aging is due to a deficiency in the quantity and quality of *succus de vitae*, to coin a phrase, which means "juice of life"—a combination of hormones and secretions of all of our endocrine glands.

Scientifically, no one can deny the dynamic influence which these secretions have upon our minds in the production of complex emotions. Mind and body can no longer be considered as divorced entities. From the moment we draw our first breath, we begin to express our feelings through various behavior reactions as a body-soul unit. From crying, fretting nail-biting, thumb-sucking, temper tantrums in childhood to impulsive decisions, elations and depressions of adolescence.

The emotional tone or the so-called "affectivity" of an individual is closely associated with the vital functions of his visceral organs. The famous Dr. Crile once said that "When stocks go down, diabetes goes up." Have you ever appreciated the effect a quarrel, or a bad-news telegram may have on your appetite? How worry is able to drag down the normal weight of an individual? How recovery from a critical illness results in a renewed determination to live?

Every doctor can relate many instances where this will to live has been a decided and perhaps the deciding factor in the recovery of a patient.

It is this very phenomenon of the influence of the mind over our body-organs that also influences our longevity. Negative thinking can curtail your life span.

▲ *Through Self-Hypnosis Henry Discovered One of the Secrets of Longevity.* Henry informed us that a few years ago he experienced what he described as the greatest frustration of his life—his greatest sorrow. His wife died of cancer at the age of 57.

Here is the story of Henry and his tragic misfortune and how self-hypnosis helped him develop a new philosophy of life.

Henry had planned to retire to Florida after 30 years of married life. He and his wife made extensive preparations for the building of their "dream-house" where they would spend their remaining years in comfort. Henry's wife was an accomplished artist, and she planned to devote full time to painting. Henry on the other hand, a retired engineer, took courses in woodwork. He made this his hobby and thought he would find enjoyment and serenity in making frames for his wife's paintings, plus other woodworking activities. He longed to do something with his hands, to overcompensate for the many years he devoted to mental or "brain-work" as he put it.

He looked forward to living out his life in a warm climate, in a beautiful home, equipped with a studio for his wife and a workshop for himself.

But Fate struck a cruel blow. His wife was stricken with a gall bladder attack and within three months succumbed to cancer. Henry's world had come to an end. He died emotionally. Nothing was of interest to him. He had become 20 years older than his calendar years.

His sister, who was deeply concerned about him, suggested that he consult a psychiatrist. Henry became depressed, lonely and had lost his will to live.

Following several interview consultations, he consented to learn how he might help himself with techniques of self-hypnosis. We acquainted him with such terms as autorelaxation, autoanalysis, and autotherapy. We explained how self-hypnosis works, and what he had to do to make self-hypnosis successful.

At this point we would like him to describe in his own words the results he obtained:

> I kept repeating to myself, using the method of hypnotic self-suggestion, that I had much to live for, that I had to carry on in memory of my beloved wife (for that is the way she would have wanted it), to continue discharging responsibilities to my children. Self-analysis, self-relaxation, self-hypnosis were terms that seemed meaningless to me, but patiently and with understanding these powerful aids were explained to me. During the sessions that followed

I gradually began to dispel my feelings of self-pity and finally concluded that to succumb to grief was abnormal and fruitless. While I realized that the source of my former happiness could not be regained, I could at least, by changing my attitude, seek peace of mind. I thereby resolved to make myself useful, to offer a hand to others who seemed in more desperate need of help. A more cheerful pattern on my part succeeded in overcoming irritable selfish tendencies and anxieties that were insidiously manifesting themselves. I began to find satisfaction in doing odd repair jobs for my friends, in helping children with their school work, in vocational guidance, in giving talks on some of the latest achievements and in making useful to others some of the knowledge gained in almost four decades of specialty in my profession. I began to read books I wanted so much to read, but for which it seemed I could never find the time. I found enjoyment in listening to good music, in watching television and in more closely following world developments. I would save the editorial section of the Sunday papers so that I could peruse the news more intelligently during the week. I would clip poetry and illustrations that I knew would have pleased my wife. Her paintings in my room became a source of inspiration to me and afforded the required courage to carry on. I decided to go to Europe with my sister and there I saw the places and people I wanted to see. Gradually I was acquiring a changed and healthy attitude of life. I was becoming younger instead of older. I had not realized that the right outlook could overcome my misfortune. I told myself repeatedly that I *could* survive this great disappointment in my life.

After a long period of adjustment through self-hypnosis and self-analysis, I began to see rays of hope and life had a meaning again. I had learned to live alone, I was making new friends. No longer did I dread solitude and old age. I was accepting my destiny without complaint. When periods of depression arose, I would seek relief in self-hypnosis. I would think of my children and grandchildren, how happy they were to see me coming to their homes. I would think of the happy days spent in Boy Scout activities where I observed the eagerness of youth in the pursuit of knowledge and of service to others. In brief, I replaced *negative* thinking with *positive* and *optimistic* thoughts. I would not allow myself to fall again a victim of self-pity. I truly began to relax and take things in their stride as they occurred each day. I was finding peace with myself at last. Utilizing the power of self-hypnosis enabled me to adjust myself intelligently, unemotionally and healthfully to what I had feared was my greatest life's frustration. I overcame my sorrow with repeated suggestions that I could live out my remaining years fruitfully by helping others, by maintaining my faith in the goodness of other people in the world. I am also planning on re-marrying.

I am confident that as long as I can continue to enjoy this peace, as long as I remind myself of the saving power of the human mind I shall never grow old in the true sense of the word.

Let your work become your hobby

Many people are bored with life because life is drudgery to them. They remind themselves how much they dislike their work, how they hate going to work, how tired they are after eight hours at their job. These same people complain even when they change their job. Nothing ever seems to satisfy them. Many of them are chronic complainers. They are victims of a *sick* attitude about everything. But this can be changed. Self-hypnosis is a technique for changing yourself by changing your attitude. Once you accomplish this all life takes on a different perspective. You begin to feel healthier, happier and less tired.

Here is some excellent advice from Dr. Alfred J. Cantor, a physician-author, who substantiates from his own experience what we have just said.

Simplify life by letting your work become your hobby. Learn to like what you do to the point where you look upon it as a hobby. Again, it is merely a matter of attitude. As a physician I see a great many patients. Many of these patients ask me why I work so hard, or how I keep up the pace.

The answer is very simple: "I never work. I enjoy what I do." You see—it is a matter of attitude.

If you have the proper attitude, you can be active practically 20 hours a day with only four hours' sleep—and yet honestly say that you "never work." You must learn to enjoy what you do to such an extent that you are happiest when you are busy. But you are not at work.

When you have achieved this goal at the end of a very busy day, you will be full of pep and energy, raring to go. Otherwise, you may work a six- or eight-hour day—doing something you don't enjoy—and be extremely tired and be ready only for bed at the end of that short day.

If boredom and fatigue are interrelated why allow yourself to become bored? Enthusiasm dispels boredom. Enthusiasm is something that can be developed through self-hypnosis or more specifically through the technique of self-suggestion. The *right attitude* toward everything you do makes everything a lot easier.

Hypnosis and religion

According to a recent newspaper item, the 47-year-old Rev. J. Douglas Gibson, pastor of the First Methodist Church, Conyers, Georgia, has been using hypnosis to help his subjects in solving problems. He has found it a helpful aid in counseling some 200 persons. The Reverend Gibson states that he "often has been able during the past two years to penetrate a 'wall of resistance' which prevents many individuals from responding to everyday counseling techniques."

By bypassing the conscious mind in difficult cases, Rev. Gibson states he "not only gets at the seat of problems more directly, but also can help to achieve more effective solutions."

Self-hypnosis makes prayer more effective

Dr. William J. Bryan has recently written an excellent book entitled *Religious Aspects of Hypnosis* (Springfield, Ill.: Charles C. Thomas, Publisher). It contains a Foreword by Dr. S. J. Van Pelt, President of the British Society of Medical Hypnotists.

Dr. Bryan attempts to show how prayer is akin to a state of hypnosis and how the prophets produced visions by hypnosis: "Prayer is a state of mind, an altered state of consciousness, a specific kind of hypnosis. The conversation of prayer is merely the communication between the mortal and his God."

As to whether our prayers are answered, Dr. Bryan writes:

> The fact that millions of individuals actually receive what they pray for supports the idea that if what one prays for is genuinely good for him, and if the prayer in itself is in earnest and properly executed, it will, quite amazingly be frequently answered in the affirmative.

He adds:

> In order to receive the affirmative answer to one's prayer it is important to *believe*. This can only be accomplished when it is done on a level of deep emotion within the recesses of the deepest parts of our mind and soul. This "sincere true belief" is only felt by the employment of hypnosis.
>
> The prophets produced their visions by a form of auto-hypnosis, and in the Middle Ages most of the prophets who heard the voice of God actually dissociated their own voices and heard themselves. The visions of Ezekiel and Daniel were definitely produced by auto-hypnosis and men were shown in dreams what was suggested to them by their own thoughts.

In another section of his book Dr. Bryan points out,

> Many theologians of that era used auto-hypnosis to deepen
> their own religious experience enabling them to remain
> closer to their own personal Gods. Many elements of hyp-
> nosis remain in our religion today. The chanting, testi-
> monials, the flickering candles and the cross as a fixation
> point for our vision; the relaxation of the rest of our body;
> the bowing of our heads in supplication; the silence in the
> Friend's meeting; Kavanah in Jewish mysticism; the Prep-
> aration for prayer; the rotation of the body in the syna-
> gogue, and the effect of prayer on those who offer it, are
> all examples of hypnotic techniques which have been ac-
> cepted as part of our own religious experience.

We are very pleased to know that there are those who recognize the value of what we might call the "hypnotic approach."
A clergyman needs to develop a hypnotic personality—radiating
positive rapport with his parishioners. He must give them a feeling of comfort, a feeling of relaxation, a feeling of confidence.
The *new approach* has no place for shouting, threatening ser-
mons. People are seeking peace of mind. They don't want to be
frightened and made to feel guilty. The voice of the pastor must
be soothing as the organ music. His Sunday message must bring
comfort and hope to those in need of spiritual encouragement.
More people would attend church regularly if clergymen would
use their hypnotic powers to dispel people's fears and supersti-
tions. Instilling the fear of Hell for the punishment of our sins
is a *negative* approach.

Autohypnosis recognizes the existence of God-Power in all of
us. It is allied to Mind-Power, a force for good. It enables us to
overcome fear, to survive personal misfortunes and inspire courage in others. God-Power is a self-healing power.

Self-hypnosis should help you supplement your Sunday
church religion with an *inner religion*, a seven-day-a-week religion
—a religion of LOVE WITHOUT FEAR—a religion of POSI-
TIVE THINKING.

Prayer becomes more effective when self-hypnotic techniques are employed. The person who has achieved self-mastery through self-hypnosis is better able to experience inner peace, because he believes and has faith in the power of love that exists within him.

Autohypnosis and church-religions have common goals—self-improvement, via positive suggestions, self-forgiveness, love of our fellowman, faith in mankind and a belief in a Higher Power, a Divine Power that is omnipotent.

Self-hypnosis can make you more amenable to the help which you seek from your particular church-religion.

I believe

The following are a few *pre-sleep thoughts* to give your subconscious mind each night after you have finished your prayers.

Jot them down on a small card and carry it with you all the time in your pocket or purse. Before long you will have acquired a new way of thinking—a better way of living.

By getting into the habit of repeating them to yourself night after night you are instilling the essence of all religions into your subconscious mind. This technique of autosuggestion through autohypnosis gives you inner religion—a soul religion—a lifelong philosophy of life—a rock of Gibraltar *faith* in yourself.

1. *I believe* that life with all its complications and hardships is worth living.
2. *I believe* in the existence of a Higher Power, a Force of Love, that is eternal, that puts meaning into our lives.
3. *I believe* that I have the mind-power to survive all life's frustrations, disappointments and misfortunes.
4. *I believe* that I have the capacity to acquire and experience inner peace of mind.
5. *I believe* that happiness comes from the ability to enjoy life and an unselfish desire to comfort and help others.
6. *I believe* that I am capable of improving my life by improving my way of thinking.

7. *I believe* that I can give love, accept love and share love.

8. *I believe* that I can conquer any habit that is detrimental to my health.

9. *I believe* that I can apply all that I have learned about myself and my subconscious mind toward making my life more successful.

10. *I believe* that life is what I make it, that I am master of my fate.

Remember that these are new attitudes which you are going to achieve and adopt. Label them "Daily Reminders." Carry the card with you in your wallet or purse as you would your driver's license, identification or social security card. Refer to it daily. Soon you will be carrying out these printed self-given suggestions until you have them memorized. They can change your entire life from an old to a new and better way of thinking and living.

What to remember

Self-hypnosis can help you develop the art of living a long, happy life. How? By giving yourself these posthypnotic suggestions. Believe them. Memorize them. Put them into practice:

1. I am going to regain my zest for life.
2. I am going to make my own age.
3. Old age is conceived in the mind.
4. I am going to observe moderation in everything I do.
5. I am going to see my doctor regularly for periodic check-ups.
6. I am going to remain young in mind and heart by finding new pleasures, new interests, new friends.
7. I am going to learn to laugh more.
8. My goal in life shall not merely be a longer life, but a richer one.
9. I am going to make my golden years interesting and meaningful.

10. I am going to practice relaxation as a way of life.

11. I am not going to be a stay-at-home just because I am past 60 or even 70.

12. Growing old graciously means practicing being kind, unselfish and understanding.

13. Worry, doubts, fears and tensions only deepen the wrinkles of age.

14. I am going to learn to grow wiser as I grow older.

15. A love of life, a gladness to be alive, a will to live, will keep me young forever.

Chapter Fifteen

Richer living through
new thought patterns

▲ We recommend that you put into practice what you have learned in this book. You will soon prove to yourself that life with all its varied complications can be very rewarding—that life is worth living—that you can learn to become master of your fate through self-hypnosis.

In order to reassure ourselves that you will achieve whatever you had hoped to achieve from reading this book, let us summarize in this final chapter the important things we recommend that you keep in mind.

First of all, you have an advantage over the average person insofar as you have been educated into knowing the *facts* about hypnosis. You have dispelled from your mind *fallacies* which would hamper you from benefiting from self-hypnosis. You know that self-hypnosis is a force for good, that there is nothing to fear from making good use of it. You can always rouse yourself from the hypnotic state. We also suggested in our early chapters that you exercise good judgment in consulting your physician or psychiatrist if there is any doubt in your mind as to whether your symptoms require medical attention or whether some deep-seated emotional problem requires special management by a psychiatrist. We have found that giving our readers such advice is *essential*. We do not wish to convey the impression that self-hypnosis is a cure-all for anything and everything. By citing examples of conditions that responded favorably to self-hypnosis, we have shown quite specifically when self-hypnosis can be used effectively.

You should be convinced by now that self-hypnosis has unlimited potentialities. One of the most valuable benefits lies in the discovery of your inner self. Self-hypnosis should enable you to develop self-respect and self-confidence. It serves as a powerful weapon against self-defeatism.

Now that you have learned the 4-A's method of self-hypnosis, apply it to specific problems. You will find that there will be nothing you cannot solve or correct. You'll experience personality-maturity. You will learn to become immune to frustration. Your sense of values will be better. You will automatically find yourself becoming the kind of a person you want to be. You will make better use of your time. Your thinking will be more systematized.

Self-hypnosis helps you develop self-discipline. It is a *self-teaching technique* for achieving your goals in life. By improving your *inner you*, through the better understanding of the subconscious, you experience a more successful relationship with other people.

Anyone can attain self-hypnosis only because we are all *suggestible*—capable of being influenced by our own thinking. You remember we described hypnosis as a state of heightened suggestibility. When you induce the hypnotic state you are merely making yourself more *receptive* to suggestion—more receptive to *positive thinking* by utilizing the power of the subconscious mind. Self-hypnosis makes use of conscious autosuggestion. But it goes a step beyond conscious thinking. It puts the subconscious mind to work, enabling it to accept and act on suggestions given to it by the conscious mind. Through self-hypnosis you can harness the potential and the force of the subconscious for constructive living. *This is the one great advantage over all other therapeutic methods of self-improvement.*

Self-hypnosis makes self-improvement a *lifelong habit.* You improve despite yourself. New thought patterns become a conditioned reflex. You change for the better *automatically.* Once you plant a seed in the ground it grows by itself. You can help it to grow faster by fertilizing the soil. Once you plant a thought in the subconscious mind it develops by itself into what might be called a *conditioned habit.*

One way of reminding your subconscious mind of the tremendous benefits derived from the use of self-hypnosis is to read and reread the table of contents. It will serve more or less as a summary of the entire book. In one of your sessions, after you are in the hypnotic state, try to review and memorize the essential substance of each chapter. In this way we guarantee that you will be getting the maximum value of the book.

You and heredity

One of the most unfortunate and damaging fallacies that people still harbor is that nervousness, alcoholism, insanity, temper tantrums are inherited. Even those who have been enlightened by scientific knowledge and perhaps admit that these conditions are not really inherited, according to books they've read, handicap themselves by worrying about "hereditary influences," what psychiatrists sometimes refer to as "hereditary predispositions."

We *imitate* consciously or unconsciously the traits of our parents, their way of thinking and doing things. In identifying ourselves with one or both parents we grow up to be like them, not because of heredity but because of being exposed to their influences over the years. When we become adults we have an opportunity to re-evaluate our parents in terms of personality-assets and personality-liabilities.

We no longer need to feel discouraged, thinking that we are

chips off the old block—that "There's nothing I can do about the way I am," that "I must have taken after my father or my mother." We can change and modify those influences we attribute to our parents. Blaming our parents serves merely as a rationalization for not wanting to change ourselves for the better. It's nothing more than an alibi.

In attempting to achieve greater self-understanding through self-hypnosis we can allow ourselves to regress to childhood and re-live our early emotional relationship to our parents. Insight as to the origin of our present shortcomings can be very helpful. But in psychoanalyzing our parents in our amateur way we must suggest to ourselves during self-hypnosis that we are going to be forgiving, that we are not going to nurse resentments against our parents, that we can undo any harm they might have done, that we can become our new self by being *unlike* our parents, if need be. We can acquire an entirely new personality via the method of self-suggestion.

It is comforting to have an eminent physician-writer like Dr. Walter Alvarez confess that he too was once a victim of a false belief about heredity.

The following appeared on the jacket of his book *Live At Peace With Your Nerves* (Prentice-Hall, Inc., 1958):

> When I was a young man (Dr. Alvarez admits) I feared that I would not amount to much because I had inherited my mother's nervousness and fatigability. I resolved that I would try to do the many wise and useful things my mother did, but avoid doing all the unwise things that wasted her strength and time.
>
> Obviously, my transformation did not come about overnight, but only after years of self-discipline. By hoarding my energies, I found enough strength for two jobs—one earning a living and the other doing research, writing, teaching and lecturing. I even had energy left over for a few hobbies, like mountain climbing, photography and book collecting.

Once again we like to emphasize that the power of self-mastery lies with us. We have the mind-power to become what we want to be irrespective of heredity, our family background, early environmental influences or what have you. You can suggest away the habit notion that you are what your parents made you. Give yourself the suggestion instead that: "I am captain of my soul, I can achieve self-mastery through positive thinking, through self-hypnotic suggestions."

Making the most of each day

There is much that can be said for the philosophy "Live one day at a time." Wallowing in past regrets, or worrying about the future is wasted energy. People should concentrate on the *present*. We don't wish to contradict ourselves. Making plans for tomorrow, the next day and the next is wise, but we must not forget that unless we start *today* with our self-improvement resolutions, the future will not be what we had hoped it to be. Tomorrow is dependent upon what we do today. We need to discipline ourselves to enjoy each moment of living. We don't know what tomorrow will bring. Self-hypnosis techniques can help you develop that feeling of being glad to be alive, that feeling that each new day is an interesting day, a day of growing, believing, a day of hope.

We recently came across a small paperback book entitled *Living Each Moment* by Ken Treiber. We had the pleasure of being introduced to the author and, much to our amazement, we learned that he is an engineer by profession. In our conversation with him, he told us that he practiced what he wrote. He was happy and enjoyed life, was inspired to tell others how he discovered this new found happiness. We would like to pass on to our readers a few of the things he advocates and recommend that our readers incorporate them into their self-hypnosis sessions.

Here is his formula for happiness:

1. Obtain and maintain the best health possible.
2. Be honest.
3. Pay strict attention to the moment.
4. Have wholehearted interest in others.
5. Look for the good in everyone.
6. See each person as a precious being.
7. Be agreeable, not contrary.
8. Think about others rather than self.
9. Use the word "we" rather than "I."
10. Keep an "open mind."
11. Don't be insulted if people disagree with you.
12. Let nothing disturb you.
13. Use your time wisely.

According to his diagram for achieving happiness, he claims if a person follows these rules they will possess,

1. Inward peace
2. Ability to adjust to environment
3. Joy of accomplishment
4. Success

which in turn will result in happiness.

There must be many others like Treiber who have discovered for themselves that they can have the kind of life they desire, a life inspired by achievements, a life of pleasantness and happiness.

Living can be simplified. You merely need to accept certain basic truths, certain fundamental commonsense rules and utilize self-hypnosis as a means of putting these rules of healthier living into daily practice. If you begin today—now—the future will take care of itself. You can formulate your own rules for better living. Let them become part of a morning prayer which you recite to yourself at the beginning of each new day.

Your own experience will be your best proof that self-hypnosis can accomplish wonders for you.

Twenty-five guaranteed dividends

Twenty-five guaranteed dividends from the use of self-hypnosis you can expect and are entitled to—if you follow carefully all of the instructions in the book:

1. It can change your way of living.
2. It can help you develop good health-habits.
3. It can help you break bad habits.
4. It can help you reduce and achieve normal weight control.
5. It can help you stop smoking, or smoke in moderation.
6. It can help you stop drinking, or drink in moderation.
7. It can help you overcome insomnia.
8. It can teach you to do everything the relaxed way.
9. It can help you overcome nervous tension.
10. It can help you eliminate chronic tiredness.
11. It can help you defeat mental depression and unhappy moods.
12. It can enable you to achieve greater sex-happiness in marriage and make your marriage a success.
13. It can help you solve specific sexual problems, such as frigidity, impotence and sexual aberrations.
14. It can help you find love, accept love, give love and share love.
15. It can help you develop a sense of humor so essential to happier living.
16. It can help you enjoy life.
17. It can help you make more money and attain greater success in life.
18. It can help you control your emotions and relax away sick emotions such as anger, hate, selfishness, jealousy, vanity and fear.
19. It can help you overcome feelings of inferiority and attain greater self-confidence.

20. It can give you a new lease on life.

21. It can help you get along better with people.

22. It can help you get along with yourself by acquiring a new personality.

23. It can help you stay young and live longer.

24. It can help you develop peace of mind—something we all desire.

25. It can help you develop a philosophy of life—that life at its worst is a fascinating experience—that it is wonderful to be alive—that people are basically good—that the world is improving—that we have the right to survive and enjoy life—that we have the right to be happy—that we *want, can, must,* and *will* achieve BETTER HEALTH, GREATER HAPPINESS AND MORE SUCCESS.

A reinforced suggestion

We suggested in our introduction that you can achieve many wonderful things with self-hypnosis. Now that you have completed reading the book, we hope you have been thoroughly convinced that self-hypnosis can change your way of life, that you can become a healthier, happier person. However, we would like to be *reassured* that you have benefited from the contents of the book and recommend that you *reinforce* the following suggestions during one of your self-hypnotic therapy sessions:

I was told at the beginning of the book that everyone has the capacity for self-improvement. Now that I have learned the technique of self-hypnosis I will use it for the rest of my life as a valuable means of maintaining successful self-discipline.

I intend to use it to help me achieve increasing emotional maturity and lasting peace of mind.

This book has given me the formula for happiness and success.

I am going to read this book as many times as is necessary so that I can apply wisely the knowledge that I have gained.

I am going to discover for myself that I have the power within me to control and influence my mind at will, that I can quickly convert negative thinking into positive thinking.

Each day I am to remind myself that I am

Master of my Fate
Captain of my Soul.

Epilogue

━━━━━━━━━━━━━━━━━━━━━━━━━━━━━━━━━━━━━━

▲ We predict techniques in hypnosis and self-hypnosis will occupy an important place in our daily lives in the not-too-distant future.

J. B. S. Haldane, a famous British scientist, obviously shares this same point of view, as evidenced by his statement:

> Anyone who has seen even a single example of the power of hypnosis and suggestion must realize that the face of the world and the possibilities of existence will be totally altered when we can control their effects and standardize their application.

We believe that hypnosis has potentials that are unlimited and is destined to become a great force in our society. Most people will, in the future, be practicing the techniques of self-hypnosis, for the breaking of bad habits, the control of one's emotions, the improvement of one's health and personality and the accomplishment of our various goals in life.

Self-hypnosis will become the MASTER KEY TO SUCCESSFUL LIVING.

Bibliography

Albert, Dora, *You're Better Than You Think*, Englewood Cliffs, New Jersey: Prentice-Hall, Inc., 1957.

Alvarez, Walter C., M.D., *Live at Peace With Your Nerves*, Englewood Cliffs, New Jersey: Prentice-Hall, Inc., 1958.

Anderson, Camilla M., *Beyond Freud, A Creative Approach to Mental Health*, New York: Harper and Bros., 1957.

Arons, Harry, *Handbook of Self-Hypnosis*, Irvington, New Jersey: Power Publishers, 1959.

Baudouin, C., *Suggestion and Autosuggestion*, New York: Dodd, Mead & Co., 1922.

Bernheim, H., *Suggestive Therapeutics*, New York: London Book Co., 1947.

Bramwell, J. M., *Hypnotism, Its History, Practice and Theory*, Philadelphia: J. B. Lippincott Co., 1903.

Brean, Herbert, *How to Stop Smoking*, New York: Pocket Books, Inc., 1954.

Brenman, M. and Gill, M., *Hypnotherapy*, New York: International Universities Press, 1947.

Bristol, Claude M., *The Magic of Believing*, Englewood Cliffs, New Jersey: Prentice-Hall, Inc., 1957.

Brooks, C. H., *The Practice of Autosuggestion by the Method of Emile Coué*, New York: Dodd, Mead & Co., 1922.

Brown, H., *Advanced Suggestion*, New York: William Wood & Co., 1919.

Bryan, William J., *American Institute of Hypnosis Training Manual Course No. 101.*

Burkhart, Roy A., *The Freedom to Be Yourself*, Englewood Cliffs, New Jersey: Prentice-Hall, Inc., 1956.

Caldwell, Ernest, *How You Can Stop Smoking Permanently*, Hollywood, California: Wilshire Book Co., 1960.

Caprio, Frank S., M.D., *Helping Yourself With Psychiatry*, Englewood Cliffs, New Jersey: Prentice-Hall, Inc., 1959.

———, *Sex and Love*, Englewood Cliffs, New Jersey: Parker Publishing Co., 1959.

———, *The Sexually Adequate Male*, New York: Citadel Press, 1952.

———, *The Sexually Adequate Female*, New York: Citadel Press, 1953.

———, *Marital Infidelity*, New York: Citadel Press, 1953.

———, *Living in Balance*, New York: Medical Research Press, 1951.

———, *The Power of Sex*, New York: Citadel Press, 1952.

———, *Sexual Behavior: Psycholegal Aspects* (co-authored with Brenner, Donald, LL.B.), New York: Citadel Press, 1961.

Coué, Emile, *Self-Mastery Through Conscious Autosuggestion*, New York: American Library Service, 1922.

———, *How to Practice Suggestion and Autosuggestion*, New York: American Library Service, 1922.

Crowe, John H., *You Can Master Life*, Englewood Cliffs, New Jersey: Prentice-Hall, Inc., 1954.

Duckworth, John, *How to Use Auto-Suggestion Effectively*, Hollywood, California: Wilshire Book Co., 1960.

Dudley, Geoffrey A., *How to Understand Your Dreams*, Hollywood, California: Wilshire Book Co.

Dunlap, K., *Habits, Their Making and Unmaking*, New York: Liveright, 1933.

Elman, Dave, *Reference Notes for the Course in Medical Hypnosis*, 56 Edgewood Ave., Clifton, New Jersey.

Erickson, Milton, M.D., and Cooper, Lynn F., M.D. *Time Distortion in Hypnosis*, Baltimore: Williams and Wilkins, 1959.

———, *A Seminar on Hypnosis.*

Estabrooks, George, *Hypnotism*, New York: E. P. Dutton & Co., 1957

Forel, A., *Hypnotism*, New York: Allied Publications, 1927.

Funk, Wilfred, and Lewis, Norman, *30 Days to a More Powerful Vocabulary*, New York: Wilfred Funk, Inc., 1942.

Germain, Walter B., *The Magic Power of Your Mind*, Englewood Cliffs, New Jersey: Hawthorn Publishing Co., 1956.

Giblin, Lee, *How to Have Confidence and Power Dealing With People*, Englewood Cliffs, New Jersey: Prentice-Hall, Inc., 1956.

Gutwirth, Samuel W., *You Can Learn to Relax*, Hollywood, California: Wilshire Book Co.

Hart, Hornell, *Autoconditioning*, Englewood Cliffs, New Jersey: Prentice-Hall, Inc., 1956.

Heise, Jack, *How You Can Play Better Golf Using Self-Hypnosis*, Hollywood, California: Wilshire Book Co., 1960.

———, *How You Can Bowl Better Using Self-Hypnosis*, Hollywood, California: Wilshire Book Co., 1961.

———, *The Painless Way to Stop Smoking*, Manhasset, New York: Channel Press, Inc., 1962.

Heyer, G., *Hypnosis and Hypnotherapy*, London: C. W. Daniel Co., 1931.

Hilger, W., *Hypnosis and Suggestion*, New York: The Rebman Co., 1921.

Hill, Napoleon, *Think and Grow Rich*, Sydney: Angus and Robertson, 1959.

Hollander, Bernard, *Methods and Uses of Hypnosis and Self-Hypnosis*, Hollywood, California: Wilshire Book Co., 1957.

———, *Hypnotism and Suggestion in Daily Life, Education and Medical Practice*, New York: G. P. Putnam's Sons, 1910.

Janet, P., *Psychological Healing*, New York: Macmillan Co., 1925.

———, *Principles of Psychotherapy*, New York: Macmillan Co., 1924.

Kennedy, Joseph A., *Relax and Live*, Englewood Cliffs, New Jersey: Prentice-Hall, Inc., 1953.

King, Nard, *Self-Hypnosis. A Guide to Its Wonders*, Newfoundland, New Jersey: Verity Publications, 1957.

Kingsbury, George C., *The Practice of Hypnotic Suggestion*, Hollywood, California: Wilshire Book Co., 1959.

Kinnear, Willis H., *The Creative Power of Mind*, Englewood Cliffs, New Jersey: Prentice-Hall, Inc., 1957.

Kotkin, Leonid, and Kerner, Fred, *Eat, Think and Be Slender*, Hollywood, California: Wilshire Book Co., 1960.

Kuhn, Leslie and Russo, Salvadore, *Modern Hypnosis*, Hollywood, California: Wilshire Book Co., 1958.

Laird, Donald A. and Laird, Eleanor C., *Sound Ways to Sound Sleep*, New York: McGraw-Hill Book Co., 1959.

Le Cron, Leslie M. and Bordeaux, J., *Hypnotism Today*, New York: Grune and Stratton, 1947.

Magonet, Philip, A.M.D., *Hypnosis in Medicine*, Hollywood, California: Wilshire Book Co.

Maltz, Maxwell, M.D., *Psycho-Cybernetics*, Englewood Cliffs, New Jersey: Prentice-Hall, Inc., 1960.

Marks, R. W., *The Story of Hypnotism*, New York: Prentice-Hall, Inc., 1947.

McBrayer, James T., *Hypnotism Simplified*, Baltimore, Maryland: Ottenheimer Publishers, 1956.

Morrison, Lester M., *The Low-Fat Way to Health and Longer Life*, Englewood Cliffs, New Jersey: Prentice-Hall, Inc., 1958.

Oakley, Gilbert E., *Self-Confidence Through Self-Analysis*, Hollywood, California: Wilshire Book Co.

Orton, Louis, *Hypnotism Made Practical*, Hollywood, California: Wilshire Book Co.

Peale, Norman V., *The Power of Positive Thinking*, Englewood Cliffs, New Jersey: Prentice-Hall, Inc., 1952.

———, *A Guide to Confident Living*, Englewood Cliffs, New Jersey: Prentice-Hall, Inc., 1948.

Powers, Melvin, *Advanced Techniques of Hypnosis*, Hollywood, California: Wilshire Book Co., 1957.

———, *Self-Hypnosis, Its Theory, Technique and Application.*

———, *A Practical Guide to Self-Hypnosis*, Hollywood, California: Wilshire Book Co., 1961.

———, *Mental-Power Through Sleep-Suggestion.*

———, *Hypnotism Revealed.*

Powers, Melvin, *Dynamic Thinking, The Technique of Achieving Self-Confidence and Success.*

———, Starrett, Robert S., *A Practical Guide to Better Concentration,* Hollywood, California: Wilshire Book Co., 1962.

Prince, M., *The Unconscious,* New York: Macmillan Co., 1929.

Quackenbos, J. D., *Hypnotic Therapeutics in Theory and Practice,* New York: Harper, 1908.

Reilly, William J., *How to Get What You Want Out of Life,* Englewood Cliffs, New Jersey: Prentice-Hall, Inc., 1957.

Rhodes, Raphael H., *Hypnosis, Theory, Practice and Application,* New York: Citadel Press, 1950.

Russell, Willard L., *Peace and Power Within,* Englewood Cliffs, New Jersey: Prentice-Hall, Inc., 1951.

Salter, Andrew, *What Is Hypnosis?,* New York: Farrar, Straus and Co., 1955.

Satow, L., *Hypnotism and Suggestion,* New York: Dodd, Mead and Co., 1923.

Schilder, P., *Psychotherapy,* New York: W. W. Norton & Co., 1938.

Schindler, John H., M.D., *How to Live 365 Days a Year,* Englewood Cliffs, New Jersey: Prentice-Hall, Inc. 1957.

———, *Woman's Guide to Better Living,* Englewood Cliffs, New Jersey: Prentice-Hall, Inc., 1957.

Schultz, Johannes H., *Autogenic Training,* New York: Grune and Stratton, 1959.

Schwartz, David, *The Magic of Thinking Big,* Englewood Cliffs, New Jersey: Prentice- Hall, Inc., 1959.

Simmons, Charles M., *Your Subconscious Power,* Hollywood, California: Wilshire Book Co.

Slater, Ralph, *Hypnotism and Self-Hypnosis,* Hollywood, California: Wilshire Book Co., 1956.

Sloan, H. J. and Bryan, W. J., M.D., *American Institute of Hypnosis Training Manual Course No. 102. Mental Mechanisms.*

Stekel, W., *Psychoanalysis and Suggestion Therapy,* London: Kegan, Paul, 1923.

Stevenson, George S. and Milt, Harry, *Master Your Emotions and Enjoy Living Again,* Englewood Cliffs, New Jersey: Prentice-Hall, Inc., 1959.

Taplin, A. B., *Hypnotism and Treatment by Suggestion*, Liverpool: Littlebury Bros., 1928.

Tracy, David F., *How to Sleep Without Pills*, Hollywood, California: Wilshire Book Co.

———, *Hypnosis*, New York: Sterling Publishing Co., 1952.

Tuckey, C. L., *Treatment by Hypnotism and Suggestion or Psychotherapeutics*, London: Bailliere, Tindall & Co., 1921.

Van Pelt, S. J., *Hypnotism and the Power Within*, New York: Fawcett Publications, Inc., 1956.

———, *Secrets of Hypnotism*, Hollywood, California: Wilshire Book Co., 1958.

———, Ambrose, Gordon and Newbold, George, *Medical Hypnosis Handbook*, Hollywood, California: Wilshire Book Co.

Watkins, John G., *Hypnotherapy of War Neuroses*, New York: Ronald Press, 1959.

Weitzenhoffer, Andre, M., Ph.D., *General Techniques of Hypnotism*, Hollywood, California: Wilshire Book Co.

Wetterstrand, O. G., *Hypnotism and Its Application to Practical Medicine*, New York: G. P. Putnam's Sons, 1902.

Winn, Ralph B., *Scientific Hypnotism*, Hollywood, California: Wilshire Book Co.

Wolberg, L. R., *Medical Hypnosis*, New York: Grune & Stratton, 1948.

———, *Hypnoanalysis* New York: Grune & Stratton, 1945.

Wolpe, Joseph, M.D., *Psychotherapy by Reciprocal Inhibition*, Stanford University Press, 1958.

Woodward, L. T., M.D., *Sex and Hypnosis*, Hollywood, California: Wilshire Book Co

Index

Abilities and capacities, 40-41
Advertising, 162-163
Aging, theory of, 178-182
Air travel, fear of, 127-132
Albert, Dora, 93
Alcoholics Anonymous, 85
Alcoholism, 81-86
   case studies, 85-86
   finding cause of excessive drinking, 81-86
   subconscious causes, 81-84
   symptom of personality maladjustment, 85
   use of self-hypnosis, 43, 81-86
Allport, Gordon, 146
Alvarez, Dr. Walter, 192
American Medical Association, 23
American Medical Hypnotists, 4
American Speech and Hearing Association, 55
American Weekly, The, 2, 6, 8, 113
Analysis, hypnotic self-analysis, 33-34
Anderson, Dr. Camilla M., 45
Anger, controlling, 120-122
Attitudes, changing, 146, 182-183
Autohypnosis, *see* Self-hypnosis
Autorelaxation, 27-29
   method of inducing, 27-29
   rapid method, 28-29
   used to overcome insomnia, 92
Autosuggestion, 13, 29-33
   eye closure tests, 29-30
   hand tingling test, 31-33
   swallowing test, 30-31
Autotherapy, 34, 174
   use of posthypnotic suggestions, 23, 34

Bad temper, controlling, 120-122, 165
Benefits of hypnosis, 4-5
Berger, Joseph R., 70
Bernheim, Professor H., 14
Body, power of mind over, 178-182
Braid, Dr. James, 12
Brean, Herbert, 76
Brenner, Donald, 100
British Society of Medical Hypnotists, 184
Bryan, Dr. William J., 38, 184-185

Cancer, 112-113, 122-123
Cantor, Dr. Alfred J., 182-183
Caprio, F. S., 81n, 99-100
Carnegie Institute of Technology, 160

Cautions in the use of self-hypnosis, 36
Childbirth, use of hypnosis, 4
Children, use of hypnosis, 5
Claustrophobia, curing, 124-125
Concentration, power of, 49-51
Confidence, acquiring, 4-5, 41, 161, 173
Cooper, Dr. Linn F., 158
Coué, Emile, 13
Courses in hypnotism, 37-38
Cutler, Ann, 113, 157

Daigh, Ralph, 157
Dental surgery, 4
Depressed moods, conquering, 134-143
   self-analysis of causes, 134-135
   self-hypnotic suggestions, 141-142
Diets and dieting, 57-73
   case studies, 68-73
   compulsive eating, 62
   excessive eating, 60-62
   Hypno-Diet, 60-61
   nine-step program for weight-reduction, 63-65
   obesity and emotional problems, 62-63, 72-73
   reasons for losing weight, 68-73
   use of self-hypnosis, 45, 57-73
Dorcus, Dr. Roy M., 17
Dreams, 44-46
   interpreting, 45-46
Drinking (*see* Alcoholism)

Education, use of hypnosis, 157-158
Eisenhower, Dwight David, 149
Ellis, Dr. Albert, 98, 100
Elman, Dave, 17, 38
Emergency situations and the hypnotic state, 35
Emotions, 36-37, 119-133
   factor in illness, 5-6
   obesity and, 62-63
   overcoming negative, 115
   relaxing away sick emotions, 122-123
   use of self-hypnosis to control, 119-133
Enthusiasm, 183
Erickson, Dr. Milton H., 4, 38
Eye closure tests, 29-30

Fallacies concerning hypnosis, 1-19
Fatigue, 183
   nervous, 113-114

Fear:
    controlling, 119-120
    of flying, 127-132
    of hypnosis, 16-17
    morbid, 123-126
Fleming, Thomas J., 147
Flying, fear of, 127-132
Four A's method of self-hypnosis, 25-
    39, 165
Freed, Dr. C. Charles, 112
Freud, Sigmund, 14, 177
Frigidity, 97-104
    causes, 98-99
    definition, 97
Frustrations, made an asset through
    self-hypnosis, 47-49
Funk, Wilfred, 151

Getting along with people, 159-166
Giblin, Lee, 160
Gibson, Rev. J. Douglas, 183
Girls, sexual problems, 104-105
Goals:
    happier living, 178
    listing, 40-42
Graham, Billy, 149

Habits, 146
    use of hypnosis to break undesir-
        able, 22, 58
Haldane, J. B. S., 199
Hand tingling test, 31-33
Happiness, formula for, 193-194
Harvard University, 160
Health:
    daily reminders, 58-59
    effect of sick emotions on, 122-123
    establishing good habits, 58
    posthyphnotic suggestion, 58-59
    self-hypnosis leads to better, 5-6,
        37-73
    staying young and living longer,
        177-188
    weight-control, 59-60
Heart disease, fear of, 123-124
Heise, Jack, 29n, 60-61
Hereditary influences, 191-193
Hobbies, 114-115, 182-183
Hollander, Dr. Bernard, 20
Holmes, Oliver Wendell, 118
Humor, as a tension-reducer, 117-118
Hypersuggestibility, 11
Hypno-Diet, 60-61
Hypnosis:
    acceptance by the medical profes-
        sion, 113

Hypnosis (*cont.*)
    awareness under, 17, 19
    common fallacies and facts, 15-19
    definition, 11-12
    depth of, 14
    force for good, 22-23
    how and why it works, 13-14
    hypnotic state, 12-13, 37, 190
    kinds of, 12
    nature of, 13-14
    origin of word, 12
    present-day attitude toward, 3
    self-hypnosis versus, 2-3, 19 (*see also*
        Self-hypnosis)
    theories of, 14
    use of suggestion, 13-14
Hypnotic state, 11-24, 190
    arousing self from, 35
    definition, 12-13
    misconceptions about, 15-16
Hypnotists, 3-4, 14-15
    list of, 38

Impotence, problem of, 105-107
Indian fakirs, 21
Influencing others, 159-166
Insomnia (*see* Sleeplessness)

James, T. F., 122
Johnson, Wendell, 55

Kennedy, John F., 147
Kingsbury, Dr. George C., 21
Kline, Dr. Milton V., 22-23
Kroger, Dr. William S., 112

Learning ability, 157-158
LeCron, Leslie M., 11, 38
Lewis, Norman, 151
Life
    developing new thought patterns,
        189-197
    making the most of each day, 193-
        194
Life magazine, 22
Link, Dr. Henry C., 138
Listener, being a good, 149-151
Longevity, 177-188
    posthypnotic suggestions, 187-188
    self-hypnosis and, 177-188
Love (*see also* Marriage)
    developing capacity for, 97
    effect of self-hypnosis, 8-9, 20

Marriage, 8-9, 167-176
    love life, 8-9
    making a personality-inventory, 167-
        168

Marriage (*cont.*)
  making a success of, 167-176
  sexual problems (*see* Sexual problems)
  suggestions for husbands, 170-171
  suggestions for wives, 171-172
  use of self-hypnosis, 94-108, 167-170
Marshall, Dr. Peter, 98
Maturity, effect of self-hypnosis on, 6-7
Mayo, Dr. Charles H., 138
Memory training, 157-158
Menopause, effect on personality, 137
Mental depression, 134-143
  types of, 136-138
Miles, Dr. Walter, 83
Milt, Harry, 109
Mind:
  developing mind-power, 9
  influence on life, 2
  power over body, 178-188
  subconscious (*see* Subconscious mind)
Miracles, 19
Misconceptions about hypnosis, 15-19
Moods, depressed, 134-143
Moral principles, effect of hypnosis on, 17
Morrison, Lester M., 64

Negative thinking, danger of, 130
Nervous tension (*see* Tension)
Northrup, Eric, 98

Obesity (*see also* Diets and dieting)
  emotional problems and, 62-63
Old age, 177-188
Organization of time and energy, 7-8

Pain alleviated by self-hypnosis, 22-23, 112-113
Parents:
  management of children, 175-176
  posthypnotic suggestions, 174-176
  use of self-hypnosis, 173-176
Personality, 144-158
  ability to change, 146-148
  acquiring magnetism, 149-153
  criticism of friends, 154-157
  developing a better, 144-158
  effect of mental depression on, 137-138
  effect of self-hypnosis on, 6-7, 148-149
  getting along with people, 159-166
  importance of tolerance, 153-154
  improving one's vocabulary, 151-15.

Personality (*cont.*)
  maturity, 6-7
  nature of, 144
  posthypnotic suggestions, 159-160
  traits conditioned and acquired, 145-146
  visual reminders, 165-166
Physicians, consulting, 36, 189-190
Plans and planning, 12, 41-42
  use of self-hypnosis in, 7-8
Positive thinking, 5, 189-197
  suggestions for, 139-141
Posthypnotic suggestions, 23, 34
Powers, Melvin, 3, 29n, 38, 40, 51, 61, 132
Prayer and hypnosis, 184-186, 194
  pre-sleep thoughts, 186-187
Problem-solving, use of subconscious mind, 46-49
Psychiatrists, consulting, 189-190
Psychosomatic ills, 5

Relexation and self-hypnosis, 109-118
  inducing state of self-relaxation, 27-29
  results of, 116
  in self-hypnosis, 19
Religion and hypnosis, 183-186
Resistance to hypnosis, 16-17
Rodgin, David W., 158
Roosevelt, Franklin D., 148-149

Salesmanship and self-hypnosis, 162-165
Salter, Andrew, 11
Schindler, Dr., 5
Schwartz, David J., 150
Self-discipline, 7, 33-34
Self-hypnosis:
  achieving in the waking state, 35
  advantage of having been hypnotized, 37-38
  caution in the use of, 36
  definition, 3-4, 10, 24
  effects of, 1-10
  emergency situations during, 35-36
  examples of success in using, 46-54
  4-A's method, 25-39, 165
  future of, 119
  new way to successful living, 1-10
  potentialities, 3, 10, 190
  rousing self from hypnotic state, 35
  self-induced relaxation, 19
  step-by-step plans, 25-39
  25 guaranteed dividends, 195-196
  works automatically, 23-24

Self-importance, developing feelings of, 5

Self-improvement through hypnosis, 5, 34, 191

Self-knowledge, key to self-discipline, 33-34

Self-relaxation, 109-118
  inducing state of, 27-29

Self-therapy, 34

Sessions, number required, 16

Sexual problems:
  developing capacity for love, 97
  examples of the use of self-hypnosis, 100-104
  frigidity, 97-104
  impotence, 105-107
  insight-therapy, 94
  menopause, 137
  posthypnotic suggestions, 96-97, 100
  self-analysis, 94-96
  self-hypnosis to solve, 18, 94-108, 167-170
  single girls, 104-105
  sleeplessness caused by, 89
  suggested readings, 99-100

Sleeplessness, 87-93
  causes, 87-92
  guilt feelings, 89
  how to induce restful sleep, 92
  pain and discomfort, 88-89
  posthypnotic suggestions, 93
  self-hypnotism for, 87-93
  tension-fatigue and, 88

Smoking, 74-81
  facts concerning, 74-76
  incidence of lung cancer and, 75
  motivational factor, 77
  nervous tension increased by, 75-76
  posthypnotic suggestions, 76-81
  results of breaking the habit, 75-76
  use of self-hypnosis, 43, 76-81

Speech problems, 53-55

Stage fright, overcoming, 125-126

"Stage Hypnosis," 22

Starrett, Robert, 50

Stekel, Dr. Wilhelm, 177

Stevenson, Dr. George S., 109

Students, use of self-hypnosis, 51-52

Stuttering and stammering, 53-54

Subconscious mind, 3-4, 13
  problem-solving, 46-49
  self-hypnosis and, 40-56
  study of dreams, 44-46

Suggestibility, tests for, 29-33

Suggestion:
  autosuggestion, 29-33

Suggestion (*cont.*)
  becoming receptive to, 16, 190
  daily reminders, 187
  key to hypnotism, 13-14
  posthypnotic, 19, 23, 33-34
  reinforcing, 196-197
  visual, 165-166
  voluntary acceptance of, 16, 29

Swallowing test, 30-31

Techniques of hypnosis, 14, 25-39
  achieving hypnosis in the waking state, 35
  arousing self from hypnotic state, 35
  autoanalysis, 33-34
  autorelaxation, 27-29
    rapid method of, 28-29
  autosuggestion, 29-33
  autotherapy, 34
  courses in hypnotism, 37-38
  practicing, 9

Teenagers, hypnosis used with, 5

Temper, 120-122, 165

Tensions:
  cause of insomnia, 88
  controlling reactions, 110-112
  effect of hypnosis on, 4
  humor to reduce, 117-118
  inducing state of self-relaxation, 27-29
  nervous fatigue, 113-114
  self-therapeutic suggestions, 114-115
  tension-breaking habits, 110
  unhappiness greatest cause of, 115, 118
  use of self-hypnosis, 109-118

"Think Your Fears Away," 2

Thinking, 2
  negative, 130
  positive, 5, 189-197

Time, planning use of, 41-42

Tolerance, 153-154

Tranquilizers, use of, 4

Treiber, Ken, 193-194

Van Pelt, Dr. S. J., 14, 32, 184

Visual reminders, 165-166

Vocabulary, importance of, 151-153

Weight-reduction, 59-68
  nine-step program, 63-65

Weiss, Dr. Edward, 123-124

Worry, 116-117
  acquired habit, 116

Writing, use of self-hypnosis in, 52-53

Young, ability to stay, 177-188